If you are serious about establishing your personal relationship with God, put aside your "religiosity" and experience *The Forgotten Covenant*. This book scripturally depicts the priceless treasure promised to those who understand that "we were created to be a part of something eternal." Biblical examples, as well as contemporary stories, challenge us to examine our own relationship to God.

    Dr. Debra Peppers
    Radio and television talk show host
    National Teachers Hall of Fame
    University instructor and author

This book gives simple clarity and understanding to what has been a complicated topic.

We all need to have a clear grasp of the covenant offered by the true and living God, and this book does that. It applies to all, but for many who have known the Lord for some time, it is refreshing and enlightening to see the continuity of God's plans revealed. I was provoked to recommitment in the area of intimacy with the Lord. This is an easy read that reveals the profound truth of God's overwhelming love toward us and our need to fully embrace Him.

    Vic Gerson, Pastor
    Victory Fellowship Church
    Crestwood, MO 63128

Does your life lack purpose and direction? Do you feel like you are just drifting aimlessly from day to day? Have you lost the newness, novelty, and wonder of your early Christian experience? As you read this book, be prepared to fall in love again. The thoughts expressed in it will not give you a new system of truth or a new and superior form of religion. You will discover that your life can be kept vibrant, fresh and full of impact in a loving Covenant relationship with the King of kings.

    Terry E. Brooks, Th.D
    Internationally known Bible teacher and lecturer
    Author of *Book of Revelation: Meaningful Mysteries for Today:* Dorset, England

This is a practical book that touches the reader with God's heart. By taking a covenant journey through the Bible, it strips away religious facades, giving fresh understanding of God's covenant, and drawing the reader into a deeper, more intimate walk with Jesus.

    Mike Bickle, Pastor, Author
    Director International House of Prayer
    Kansas City, MO

In a time when societies experience fear of an unstable future, this book succinctly summarizes and clarifies God's timeless good news. Uniquely weaving God's Word with contemporary examples, *The Forgotten Covenant* fosters faith in an unchangeable Covenant Partner who delights in keeping all His promises. You will hear the drum beat of God's heart, wooing you closer to His Son. This book will change you.

    Jeff Riddering, Pastor
    Victory Fellowship
    Crestwood, MO 63128

The Forgotten Covenant

*God's Key to an
Abundant Life*

The Forgotten Covenant

God's Key to an Abundant Life

J.J. WOODS

© 2003 by Jerilyn J. Woods. All rights reserved.

Printed in the United States of America

Packaged by Pleasant Word, a division of WinePress Publishing, PO Box 428, Enumclaw, WA 98022. The views expressed or implied in this work do not necessarily reflect those of Pleasant Word, a division of WinePress Publishing. Ultimate design, content, and editorial accuracy of this work are the responsibilities of the author.

No part of this publication may be reproduced, stored in a retrieval system, or transmitted in any way by any means—electronic, mechanical, photocopy, recording, or otherwise—without the prior permission of the copyright holder, except as provided by USA copyright law.

Unless otherwise noted, all Scriptures are taken from the Holy Bible, New International Version, Copyright © 1973, 1978, 1984 by the International Bible Society. Used by permission of Zondervan Publishing House. The "NIV" and "New International Version" trademarks are registered in the United States Patent and Trademark Office by International Bible Society.

Scripture references marked KJV are taken from the King James Version of the Bible.

Scripture references marked NASB are taken from the New American Standard Bible, © 1960, 1963, 1968, 1971, 1972, 1973, 1975, 1977 by The Lockman Foundation. Used by permission.

ISBN 1-57921-600-5
Library of Congress Catalog Card Number: 2003100952

Dedication

Lovingly dedicated to my grandchildren.

I have no greater joy than this, to hear of my children walking in the truth

3 John 1:4

Table of Contents

Foreword 13

Chapter 1: What Is a Covenant? 15
Chapter 2: A Covenant in Action 25
Chapter 3: The Beginning of God's Covenant 57
Chapter 4: A Covenant Partner 73
Chapter 5: The Covenant Preserved 77
Chapter 6: The Cutting of Covenant 89
Chapter 7: Trusting in God's Covenant 99
Chapter 8: Abiding in God's Covenant 111
Chapter 9: Living in the Covenant 127
Chapter 10: Walking in God's Covenant 139
Chapter 11: The Israelites Enter God's Covenant 157
Chapter 12: Honoring the Covenant 195
Chapter 13: Covenant Is Relationship 207
Chapter 14: God's Covenant Fulfilled 215
Chapter 15: The Covenant Today 239

Foreword

Writing this book has been a joy. I now humbly offer it as a gift to fellow believers, who may be struggling to live a Christian life in the midst of the everyday world, and to all who, having been hurt or disappointed by organized religion, question the very existence of a living, loving God. The answers you seek are found in God's Covenant. Understanding it is to discover a priceless, forgotten treasure.

Entering into it will change your life!

J. J. Woods

Chapter 1

WHAT IS A COVENANT?

The secret of the LORD is for those who fear Him.
He will make them know His covenant (Psalm 25:14).

I shudder to think of how close I came to missing the most powerful, life-changing discovery of my life. After months of preparing to teach a class on God's Covenant, I was ready to quit. "God, I can't do this," I cried, slamming the book closed in utter frustration. The subject appeared to be too broad, too overwhelming. It touched absolutely every area of life, yet I couldn't seem to get a handle on it. Andrew Murray once said, "To many a man, who has never thought much of the Covenant, a true and living faith in it would mean the transformation of his whole life."[1] This is exactly what I felt. Instinctively, I knew that to pursue an

---

[1] *The Two Covenants* by Andrew Murray. Used by permission of Christian Literature Crusade, 701 Pennsylvania Avenue, P.O. Box 1449, Fort Washington, PA 19034. Page 2.

understanding of Covenant would be to take a step onto holy ground and have my life forever changed. "Are you willing to take that step?" God whispered. It was a life-changing moment of decision for which I will be eternally grateful.

Months later as I sat dressed in a hospital gown waiting for the doctor to prepare another battery of tests, I felt especially blessed for having taken that step. "God, I'm frightened," I silently prayed. "I need Your strength." Had I found myself in this situation prior to reaching an understanding of the Covenant relationship, I would have bombarded heaven with a barrage of questions. Why is this happening? Am I going to be all right? How many more tests will I have to endure? But now it was enough to know that my Covenant Partner was with me, and that He would provide all I needed to walk through this frightening experience. As I waited, the loving infusion of His strength and comfort assured me that I was not alone.

Today, having taught Covenant numerous times, I realize that we have only begun to scratch the surface of understanding all God has made available to us. I have watched individuals become born again as the realization of God's Covenant dawned upon their hearts. And I have witnessed Christians shed the shackles of "religion" to walk in a new-found freedom through a clearer understanding of God's Covenant.

What is a covenant? Since God calls Christianity a covenant, we need to understand what that means; this book has been written to help you discover God's Covenant for yourself. Although the practice of blood-covenanting dates back to the beginning of recorded history, and was practiced by every civilization on earth, we in this twenty-first century remain strangely ignorant of its meaning. Webster's Dictionary defines the word *covenant* as a contract or compact. We all understand a contract to be a document which legally binds two parties to agreed-upon obligations, but one which can be negated if so desired. However, this falls so short of a biblical covenant that the two are incomparable. The biblical definition of a covenant involves the coming together of two parties, the shedding of blood, the exchanging of vows, and a sign or symbol given to serve as a reminder to the parties involved. Those entering into a covenant often erected an altar, assembled a pile of stones, or planted a tree to serve as a memorial of their vows. These vows were stronger than family ties, superseded personal ambition, promised everlasting unity, and could not be negated under any circumstances. In fact, God uses the words *everlasting* and *unchanging* to emphasize the permanence of His Covenant.

Since everything familiar to us is in a continual state of flux—growing up, growing old, wearing out, and being replaced—this permanence of God presents us with a dilemma. We may wish it to be otherwise, but we have come to expect and accept change as a normal part of life. Yet, God says, *"I, the LORD, do not change"* (Malachi 3:6) and *"Jesus Christ is the same yesterday and today, yes, and forever"* (Hebrews 13:8). How can we hope to understand this? The answer is found in His Covenant.

One of the promises of God's Covenant is that He remains forever joined to His Covenant partners. He says to them, *"I will never desert you nor will I ever forsake you"* (Hebrews 13:5). This is initially perplexing. Living as we do, responsibilities dictate that families spend hours, days, and even months apart. Still, God says that He never leaves nor forsakes those who are in Covenant with Him, not even for an instant. How can that be possible? Was He speaking literally, or was He simply being redundant for the sake of emphasis? A look at the original Greek helps us to understand this promise of God.

The Greek word translated *never* means "not at all, in no case, not in any way" (3364, Strong's Exhaustive Concordance of the Bible).

The Greek word translated *desert* means "to slacken, to let up, to loosen, to give up, to abandon (Ibid. 447).

The Greek word translated *forsake* means "to desert, to leave in a lurch, to abandon" (Ibid. 1459).

God was not being the least bit redundant. His carefully chosen words convey the depth of His love and commitment. He says to His Covenant partner, "My love for you will never diminish. I will never give up on you, leave you in a lurch, nor abandon you for any reason. In the midst of every situation, I am with you, loving you, protecting you, guiding you, and undergirding you with My strength. In the end, I will take you home to be with Me." Spouses may leave, and friends may prove unfaithful, but God forever loves and cares for the one who belongs to Him. His desire is, as it has always been, for individuals to walk with Him, sharing their lives with Him, and experiencing the incredible joy of His presence every day.

I believe there are two reasons why I initially struggled with teaching the subject of Covenant. First, my attitude needed adjusting. I thought to myself, *I know this. It will be easy.* I had to hit rock bottom and admit that I knew little, if

What Is a Covenant?

anything, about God's Covenant. Only then was my heart prepared to hear from Him. You may be the same.

Secondly, I was unaware of the fact that there is an enemy who desires to keep individuals ignorant of God's Covenant. If you are serious about pursuing God, expect opposition from this enemy of your soul. It will come wearing many disguises—distractions, responsibilities, relationships, habits, and ridicule. Notwithstanding, the most dangerous and deceptive disguise is the spirit of religion. The late Oswald Chambers warned his Bible college students about this spirit of religion when he said, "It is possible to know all about doctrine and yet not know Jesus. The soul is in danger when knowledge of doctrine out steps intimate touch with Jesus."[2] A little knowledge coupled with the spirit of religion fosters a holier-than-thou attitude. You have most likely encountered it. It is evidenced by a closed mind, an air of intolerance, and strict adherence to man-made laws. It was the spirit of religion in the form of self-righteous Scribes and Pharisees that nailed Jesus to the cross, and that spirit of religion is alive and well today.

Prior to His death, Jesus prayed for his followers, saying, *"Father, keep them in Thy name, the name which Thou hast given Me, that they may be one, even as We are one"* (John 17:11). Unfortunately, there is little unity among Christians today. Ignorance of God's Covenant, combined with the spirit of religion, continues to foster division. Turn-

---

[2] *My Utmost for His Highest* by Oswald Chambers. © 1935, Dodd Mead & Co., Renewed © 1963 by Oswald Chambers Publications Assn., Ltd. Used by permission of Discovery House Publishers, Box 3566, Grand Rapids, MI 49501. All Rights reserved. Page 229.

ing a deaf ear to the voice of Jesus, believers argue over superficial differences. Yet, there is good news! When we come to understand God's Covenant, we realize that what Jesus asked of His Father is possible. As unique individuals with personal preferences, we will naturally favor one form of worship over another. Some of us can best express our love for God through the age-old hymns, others choose to sing praise songs and dance in the aisles, while still others prefer sitting quietly with heads bowed and eyes closed. But these differences need not divide our hearts. Unity with each other, as well as with God is possible because it is something we receive through His Covenant, not something we negotiate.

In one of my Bible study classes, a discussion of the Lord's Supper revealed obvious denominational differences. The Catholic Christians believed that the wine and bread actually became the blood and flesh of Jesus, while the Protestant believers were just as adamant that it did not. Using the words of Jesus, God showed us how to defeat that divisive, religious spirit. Jesus said, *"This is My body which is given for you; do this in remembrance of Me"* (Luke 22:19). *"This is My blood of the covenant, which is to be shed on behalf of many for the forgiveness of sins"* (Matthew 26:28). *"Do this, as often as you drink it, in remembrance of Me"* (1 Corinthians 11:25). Consequently, we discovered that when we focus on Jesus, it makes no difference whether the wine and bread remains symbolic, or becomes His actual flesh and blood. We realized that our hearts were supernaturally joined by the presence of His Holy Spirit within us, making us one.

In addition to initiating division, a religious spirit also confuses religion with relationship. Most church members

What Is a Covenant?

are familiar with the Bible and believe at least in the validity of the recorded main events. Coupling this knowledge with a church membership and a smattering of good works, they call themselves "Christian," but this is a dangerous assumption to make. According to God's Word, Christianity is a Covenant relationship of the heart. Head knowledge makes one a spectator at best. For example, if you were to attend a wedding ceremony, you would listen as the couple pledged their vows, you would watch as they exchanged the rings, and you might applaud at the conclusion of the ceremony. If you then left the church assuming yourself to be the one who had gotten married, that would be absurd. Your family would have you committed to a padded cell. Yet, when it comes to Christianity, this is too often the case. We listen to preachers, teachers, parents, and priests talk about Jesus. Believing what they tell us, we attend classes, memorize facts, recite creeds, join the church, and thereby assume that we have become a Christian. Not so! The classes, memorization, and church membership are all good things, but they are external things. Without the heart's involvement, they are nothing more than meaningless, superficial, religious exercises. Unfortunately, we usually remain ignorant of our error until we hit rock bottom, where we are forced to taste those wretched sour grapes called "letting go", the loss of a loved one, a relationship, a job, a career, a home, financial security, health, and ultimately our lives. These inescapable milestones punctuate our existence and in the midst of them, we sadly discover that allegiance to religion leaves us empty and disillusioned. In angry frustration we scream, "God where are You? Where is Your strength? Where is Your comfort? Where is Your healing? Where is Your peace that is supposed to surpass all understanding?"

If this has been your experience and you have walked away from the church lamenting, "If this is all there is, forget it," I have good news for you. There is SO MUCH MORE! Jesus came to offer relationship, not religion. He offers a powerful, intimate, Covenant relationship with God that does heal broken hearts, does give peace in the midst of chaos, and does provide supernatural strength for life's tough times. It is real and it is available. Speaking of this Covenant through the prophet Jeremiah, God said, *"Behold the days are coming when I will make a new covenant with the house of Israel and with the house of Judah* (Jeremiah 31:31). *"I will be their God and they shall be My people"* (Jeremiah 31:33). *"I will forgive their iniquity, and their sin I will remember no more"* (Jeremiah 31:34). Referring to Jesus in his letter to the Hebrews, Paul wrote, *"He is the mediator of a New Covenant"* (Hebrews 9:15, 12:24). And this New Covenant, called Christianity, is a Covenant of the heart. It is all about relationship, not religion. Jesus spoke against religious, rote behavior in Matthew 15:8–9 when He said, *"This people honors Me with their lips, but their heart is far away from Me. But in vain do they worship Me, teaching as their doctrines the precepts of men."* As the late Oswald Chambers stated, "Many a soul begins to come to God when he flings off being religious, because there is only one Master of the human heart, and this is not religion but Jesus Christ." [3]

Entering into Covenant with God requires only one thing—a heart that sincerely wants to know Him. He prom-

---

[3] Ibid. Page 200.

What Is a Covenant?

ised, *"You will seek Me and find Me, when you search for Me with all your heart"* (Jeremiah 29:13). We come to understand the permanence of God, His Covenant, and His faithfulness more fully after we enter into Covenant with Him. This is due to the fact that the instant we become His Covenant partner, He places His Holy Spirit within us. His Holy Spirit is then present and actively involved in every aspect of our lives—loving, teaching, guiding, leading, protecting, strengthening, healing, and forever causing *"all things to work together for good to those who love God, to those who are called according to His purpose"* (Romans 8:28). It is the reality of the abundant life Jesus came to give. As Kay Arthur, international speaker, writer, and founder of Precept Bible Studies declares to her students, "Everything that touches our lives is filtered through God's fingers of love before it reaches us."

Is that to suggest that God's Covenant partners are magically immune to problems? There is no such immunity in this life. However, being in Covenant with God does guarantee that in the midst of every circumstance, God remains joined to those who belong to Him, lovingly providing everything they need. The assurance that nothing escapes His notice or catches Him off guard enables His Covenant partners to live a life marked by peace and confidence. Again, Jesus calls it the abundant life. Throughout this book, we will be looking at the lives of individuals who were in Covenant with God during biblical times. These biblical examples are seasoned with contemporary stories from individuals who are walking in Covenant with God today, demonstrating the fact that He continues to lovingly receive all those who choose to walk with Him.

The Forgotten Covenant

Because the term *covenant* is antiquated and the promises of God are unfamiliar, it is easy to give up, settling for religion rather than pursuing a personal relationship with Him. However, God promises that the one who searches for Him with all his heart will find Him. The bottom line is this: when you decide to seek God with all of your heart, there is *nothing*—not the antiquated term, the uncertainty of life, nor your initial inability to comprehend the depth of God's love and commitment—that can keep you from finding Him and experiencing the joy of this forgotten Covenant.

Chapter 2

A COVENANT IN ACTION

(Jonathan and David)

Inasmuch as God refers to Christianity as a Covenant, and since the term is unfamiliar, it will be helpful to observe a covenant relationship in action. There are many covenants recorded in Scripture, but the one which best illustrates God's concept of a covenant can be seen in the lives of Jonathan and David. Jonathan was the son of Saul, the King of Israel, while David was just a poor shepherd tending his father's flock. Through a peculiar circumstance involving a giant, Jonathan and David became friends.

The nation of Israel was being threatened by the Philistine army, led by a mighty warrior over nine feet tall, called Goliath. Goliath issued a challenge to the Israelites saying, *"Choose a man for yourselves and let him come down to me. If he is able to fight with me and kill me, then we will become your servants; but if I prevail against him and kill him, then you shall become our servants and serve us"* (1 Samuel 17:8–

9). Understandably, none of the Israelites were eager to fight against this giant. None, that is, except for David. David posed the question, *"Who is this uncircumcised Philistine, that he should taunt the armies of the living God?"* (1 Samuel 17:26). Boldly announcing that he would fight the giant, David reassured Saul, *"The Lord who delivered me from the paw of the lion and from the paw of the bear, He will deliver me from the hand of this Philistine"* (1 Samuel 17:37). Wanting to help, Saul offered David a helmet and armor, but David refused. Armed with only a stick, a sling, and five stones, he set out to face Goliath. As David approached, the giant mocked him, *"Am I a dog, that you come to me with sticks?"* (1 Samuel 17:43). With divine confidence, David declared that God was fighting this battle, *"You come to me with a sword, a spear, and a javelin but I come to you in the name of the Lord of hosts, the God of the armies of Israel, whom you have taunted. This day the Lord will deliver you into my hand . . . for the battle is the Lords 'and he will give you into our hands"* (1 Samuel 17:45–47).

The rest of the story is a familiar one. Using one stone from his sling, David struck Goliath with such force that the stone sank into his forehead. As he lay unconscious, David cut off his head and carried it back to Saul in Jerusalem. From that day forward, David remained in the house of Saul, which is how he became acquainted with Jonathan.

First Samuel 18:1 says that *"the soul of Jonathan was knit to the soul of David, and Jonathan loved him as himself."* In verse three we are told that *"Jonathan made a covenant with David."* The Hebrew word *made* used in this verse means to cut, and lets us know that there was blood involved in sealing this covenant. Throughout history covenants were sealed

A Covenant in Action

as individuals made cuts on their arms or legs and mingled their blood. Heathen societies often caught the intermingled blood in a cup and required both parties to partake of it. The Hebrew phrase "made a covenant" used in this verse is *karath b'rith*, which means, "to cut, or to make a pact by cutting flesh and passing between the pieces." This indicates that in cutting their covenant, Jonathan and David sacrificed an animal. The animal was cut in two and each half positioned on the ground opposite the other. The blood of the sacrificed animal symbolized the sacredness of the covenant, as both young men walked between the pieces of flesh. By doing so, Jonathan and David were declaring, "May the Lord kill me, if I break this covenant." Unlike many of us, they understood the sacredness of a covenant, and knew that breaking it could cost them their lives.

Usually this ceremony was followed by establishing a sign or symbol of the covenant, something that would forever remind each of them of their vow. Often, when individuals made cuts on their bodies, cinders were placed into the wounds in order to form permanent scars. These scars then served as daily reminders of their vows. At times they also exchanged gifts, planted a tree, or assembled a pile of stones as a memorial. Frequently, they shared a meal together. We see this idea carried out today in our wedding ceremonies. The exchanging of rings serves as a sign or symbol of the marriage covenant, and the ceremony is usually followed by a dinner reception where gifts are presented to the couple.

As a sign of their covenant, Jonathan and David exchanged their robes, armor, and belts. The symbolism of their exchange not only reminded Jonathan and David of their vows, but also gives us insight into the components of a covenant. Let's consider each of these individually.

THE EXCHANGING OF ROBES

Entering into a covenant relationship means that the two individuals become as one. When David put on Jonathan's robe, he was symbolically putting on Jonathan, and vice versa. From that moment on, their lives were inseparable. Everything they did reflected the sacredness of their covenant vow, a vow that was soon to be tested.

Although Saul initially loved David, his feelings changed. The people were so enamored with David, that upon his return from battle, they danced and sang, *"Saul has slain his thousands, and David his ten thousands"* (1 Samuel 18:7). This was quite a blow to Saul's inflated ego, and he responded with seething jealousy. Not only did he resent the accolades bestowed upon David, but he was concerned because God's Holy Spirit had left him and now resided with David. Previously, God had informed Saul that due to his disobedience, the kingdom would one day be taken away from him. Perhaps Saul could see the writing on the wall and realized that David was destined to replace him as king. Overcome with rage, he set out to kill David. When Jonathan learned of Saul's intentions, the moment of truth arrived. Would Jonathan honor his covenant with David, if it meant going against his father? Would he remain faithful to David, if it meant relinquishing his own right to the throne? The answer to both of these questions is "Yes!" This is where we

A Covenant in Action

see the sacredness of a covenant lived out in the lives of Jonathan and David. They were truly one. Jonathan said to David, *"If it please my father to do you harm, may the LORD do so to Jonathan and more also, if I do not make it known to you and send you away, that you may go in safety. And may the LORD be with you as He has been with my father"* (1 Samuel 20:13). Time after time Jonathan enabled David to escape Saul's wrath. The exchanging of their robes was merely an external sign of their internal bond. Their hearts had become inseparably joined, as each had "put on" the identity of the other.

Since God calls Christianity a Covenant, there must have been a time when Jesus put on our robe. Let's look at what God's Word says, *"In the beginning was the Word, and the Word was with God, and the Word was God. And the Word became flesh, and dwelt among us, and we beheld His glory, glory as of the only begotten from the Father, full of grace and truth"* (John 1:1, 14). When Jesus came into this world as an infant, He put on our robe by laying aside His divinity, and willingly accepting the limitations and vulnerability of the flesh. Scripture says that He was *"a man of sorrows and acquainted with grief"* (Isaiah 53:3). Why? Because He "put on" our robe, experiencing every pain and sorrow familiar to your heart and mine.

- He knows how it feels to be tempted. When He was hungry and weak from forty days of fasting in the wilderness, Satan tempted Him three times (Luke 4:1–13).
- Jesus knows what it is like to be homeless. He said, *"The foxes have holes, and the birds of the air have*

nests, but the Son of Man has nowhere to lay His head" (Luke 9:58).
- He knows the frustration of being misunderstood. After casting out a demon, some of the crowd mocked Him saying, *"He casts out demons by Beelzebulb, the ruler of the demons"* (Luke 11:15).
- Jesus is familiar with the sting of betrayal. He said to Peter, *"I say to you, Peter, the cock will not crow today until you have denied three times that you know me."* Later that day, as Peter was denying Jesus for the third time, a cock crowed and *"the Lord turned and looked at Peter"* (Luke 22:34, 61).
- Jesus understands the embarrassment and shame of being mocked and humiliated. *"And they stripped Him, and put a scarlet robe on Him. And after weaving a crown of thorns, they put it on His head, and a reed in His right hand; and they kneeled down before Him and mocked Him, saying, 'Hail, King of the Jews!' And they spat on Him, and took a reed and began to beat Him on the head. And after they had mocked Him, they took His robe off and put His garments on Him, and led Him away to crucify Him"* (Matthew 27:28–31).
- Jesus knows that obedience to God's Word is often difficult. In the Garden of Gethsemane, as He contemplated His imminent demise, He prayed, *"My Father, if it be possible, let this cup pass from Me"* (Matthew 26:39). Jesus was asking His Father if He could bypass the cross and usher in the Covenant some other way. Three times He prayed, saying, *"Let this cup pass from Me; yet not as I will, but as Thou*

wilt." Being well aware of the pain that awaited Him on the cross, Jesus was not eager to go there, still He embraced the will of His Father.
- Jesus empathizes when our bodies are racked with pain, because He suffered one of the most excruciating tortures ever devised by man. Humbly clothed in our robe of flesh, Jesus demonstrated that it is possible to remain faithful to God in the midst of every situation.

Christianity is a Covenant relationship requiring the participation of both parties. Therefore since Jesus put on our robe, Covenant requires that we also wear His. How do we do that? The instant we turn to God, receiving Jesus Christ as our Lord and Savior, thereby entering into Covenant with Him, He places His Holy Spirit within us. His Holy Spirit becomes the symbolic robe of Jesus, joining us eternally to Himself, so that nothing is able to sever the relationship. Referring to Jesus, John the Baptist said, *"I baptize you with water; but He will baptize you with the Holy Spirit"* (Mark 1:8). The Greek word for baptize is *baptizo* and it means, "to immerse or submerge." In other words, those who are in Covenant with God are immersed in or covered by God's Holy Spirit (the robe of Jesus). Writing to believers in Galatia, Paul said, *"for all of you who were baptized into Christ have clothed yourselves with Christ. There is neither Jew nor Greek, there is neither slave nor free man, there is neither male nor female, for you are all one in Christ Jesus"* (Galatians 3:27–28). We could extrapolate this to say that there is neither Catholic nor Protestant, for we are all one in Christ Jesus.

Entering into Covenant with God by receiving the robe of Jesus Christ changes our lives forever. Once joined to Him, everything we do involves our Covenant Partner. Perhaps that sounds intimidating. You may be thinking, "No way! I could not expose Jesus to every area of my life. I need to make some changes before coming to Him." Let me assure you that God understands. He expected that response and made provision for it. Speaking of His New Covenant, God said, *"I will give you a new heart and put a new spirit within you; and I will remove the heart of stone from your flesh and give you a heart of flesh. And I will put My Spirit within you and cause you to walk in My statutes, and you will be careful to observe My ordinances"* (Ezekiel 36:26–27). These three promises—a new heart, a new spirit, and His power causing us to keep Covenant with Him—set us free from anything that would hinder our walk with God. Let's examine these promises more closely.

A New Heart

Why do we need a new heart? God said, *"The heart is more deceitful than all else and is desperately sick; who can understand it?"* (Jeremiah 17:9). That being the case, He gives a new heart to those who enter into Covenant with Him. This new heart is described in Jeremiah 31:33: *"I will put My law within them, and on their heart I will write it; and I will be their God, and they shall be My people."* Having God's laws written upon our heart means, first of all, that we possess a wisdom beyond intellectual understanding. It is a supernatural, spiritual connection to God. Even before we know His Word for ourselves, this divine wisdom enables us to walk in obedience to Him. Secondly, it means that we have the ability to understand God's Word. Under the guidance of His Holy Spirit, Scriptures which seemed confusing or irrelevant suddenly become alive to us. Much to our amazement, we understand them and they give direction to our lives. Last, but certainly not least, we find that our new heart derives great pleasure in surrendering and sharing our everyday lives with God. It is quite the opposite of the sick, deceitful heart described by Jeremiah.

New Spirit

We have already seen that the moment we enter into Covenant with God, we become one with Him by receiving His Holy Spirit. This means that God is present with us at all times. Since the Holy Spirit is an all-powerful entity there to teach, to guide, to strengthen, to protect, to heal, and to make us one with our heavenly Father, He will not be there anonymously, although, it may take some time to recognize His voice. For instance, after entering into Covenant with God, you may find that you have a keen interest in spiritual matters. Wanting to understand and experience everything God has to offer, you read your Bible, listen to teachers, and still desire more. You may find yourself praying unceasingly, which means that you are talking informally with God throughout the day, rather than just praying before meals and at bedtime. If an ambulance passes with its siren screaming, you may be surprised to find yourself praying for that stranger in distress. When faced with temptation, you will be well aware of something much stronger than conscience operating within you, undergirding you with strength.

Another way to explain the Holy Spirit's presence is to say that there are no coincidences in the life of a Christian.

For instance, God may place a thought into your mind to telephone a friend. Being busy at the moment, you initially dismiss it. Later when the thought returns and you make the call, you discover that your friend needs help. You might read a portion of Scripture that you don't understand, and as you channel surf, your attention is drawn to a Bible teacher expounding on that particular verse. God is always at work in the lives of those who belong to Him, sometimes using a gentle, reoccurring thought, and other times speaking with an urgency that defies procrastination, as in the following story.

Renee and her husband owned a small motel in a college town. One spring afternoon Renee picked up a lounge chair, tucked a book under her arm, and headed outside. Although the winter tarp still covered the pool, it felt wonderful to be basking in the warm sunshine again. After reading for almost an hour, Renee closed her book and stood up, intending to leave. But something compelled her to remain where she was. It was not an audible voice, but a strong internal directive. Somewhat taken aback, she sat down. After a few moments, feeling rather foolish, she started to get up, but once again felt strongly impressed to remain seated. This time as she sank back into the chair, she noticed a toddler making his way into the pool enclosure. He appeared to be without a chaperone, and Renee determined to keep an eye on him, as she reopened her book. Moments later, she was startled by the sound of a splash. Looking up, she saw that the toddler had fallen, and was lying face down on top of the pool cover in nine to twelve inches of water. Jumping to her feet, Renee pulled the child to safety.

A Covenant in Action

Was this a coincidence? Absolutely not! It is just an example of how God's Holy Spirit works in the lives of those who are in Covenant with Him. What God chooses to do in your life will most likely be different from what He does in mine, but our experiences will be similar in that both of us will be cognizant of His presence.

Using lamp oil to represent the Holy Spirit, Jesus told the following parable to illustrate the necessity of being in Covenant with God.

> *Then the kingdom of heaven will be comparable to ten virgins, who took their lamps and went out to meet the bridegroom. And five of them were foolish and five were prudent. For when the foolish took their lamps, they took no oil with them, but the prudent took oil in flasks along with their lamps. Now while the bridegroom was delaying, they all got drowsy and began to sleep. But at midnight there was a shout, 'Behold the bridegroom! Come out to meet him.' Then all those virgins arose and trimmed their lamps. And the foolish said to the prudent, 'Give us some of your oil, for our lamps are going out.' But the prudent answered, saying, 'No, there will not be enough for us and you too; go instead to the dealers and buy some for yourselves. And while they were going away to make the purchase, the bridegroom came, and those who were ready went in with him to the wedding feast; and the door was shut. And later the other virgins also came, saying, 'Lord, Lord, open up for us.' But he answered and said, 'Truly I say to you, I do not know you.' Be on the alert then, for you do not know the day nor the hour. (Matthew 25:1–13)*

Notice that we cannot give the Holy Spirit to one another. As much as we would like to impart Christianity to our loved ones, it is something which they must receive for themselves. If Christianity were merely a religion, we could present our loved ones with a list of things to do in order to become a Christian. But since it is a Covenant, everyone must come to God individually, and personally enter into this relationship with Him. Those who decline His invitation will hear Jesus sadly declare, "*I do not know you.*"

Jesus said that some will protest saying "*Lord, Lord, did we not prophesy in Your name, and in Your name cast out demons, and in Your name perform many miracles?*" (Matthew 7:22). In other words, "God, we have been good, religious people. We have done a lot for You." But in reply Jesus explains,

> *Not everyone who says to Me, "Lord, Lord," will enter the kingdom of heaven, but he who does the will of My Father who is in heaven. Many will say to Me on that day "Lord, Lord, did we not prophesy in Your name, and in Your name cast out demons, and in Your name perform many miracles?" And then I will declare to them, "I never knew you; depart from Me, you who practice* lawlessness.*"*
> (Matthew 7:21–23)

This is a frightening statement. These are good people, not criminals, nor outwardly rebellious individuals. To what then was Jesus referring when He accused them of practicing lawlessness? The Greek word *lawlessness* used in this verse is *anomia* and it means, "not having known or acknowledged the law." Jesus was referring to God's Covenant law which says that no one is saved apart from entering into Covenant with Him. Jesus spoke of this in John 14:6 when He said, "*I am the way, and the truth, and the life; no one comes to the Father but through Me.*" The individuals who will cringe as Jesus says, "*I never knew you*" are those who refuse to enter into His Covenant. On the surface, their deeds look good, even religious. Their actions may be benevolent; yet, refusing to relinquish control of their lives to God, they do their own thing, motivated by their own ambition. God is neither interested nor impressed. His desire is for individuals to be joined *to* Him and to work *with* Him under the direction of His Holy Spirit. Jesus said, "*Truly, truly I say to you, unless one is born again, he cannot see the kingdom of God*" (John 3:3). Those who are joined to God in Covenant are called "born-again Christians," because they have been birthed into God's kingdom. Although, the term *born again* is scorned by society today, those who are not will hear Jesus sadly declare, "*I never knew you.*"

If you are not certain that God's Holy Spirit dwells within you, I invite you to lay this book aside and talk to Him right now. This is the most important decision you will ever make. Possibly, you have attended church all of your life and been devoutly religious, but in your heart you know that something is missing. You know that you do not have a personal, intimate relationship with Jesus Christ. Now is the time to change that. Admit that you have been settling for religion rather than pursuing a relationship with Him, or perhaps you have been so turned off by religion that you have inadvertently rejected God. Ask Him to forgive you and in your own words invite Jesus Christ into your life. The words you use are inconsequential. God will be listening to your heart.

The Power to Walk in His Statutes

Lastly, God promised to *cause* those who belong to Him to keep His Covenant. What an awesome promise! We need not struggle to keep Covenant with God because He has assumed that responsibility for us. The word "cause" in Hebrew is *asah* and it is used in Scripture to describe God's creative ability. This means that any part of your life and mine that is initially out of step with God will be changed by the power of His Holy Spirit. If we postpone our coming to Him until we feel that we have cleaned up these areas, we will never come. God made it clear that under the conditions of His Covenant, it is His Holy Spirit's responsibility to change the lives of those who belong to Him, enabling them to remain faithful to His Covenant. Change is not realized by our resolutions to do better. It simply and miraculously occurs at the fusion of God's faithfulness and our obedience. As the late Oswald Chambers so succinctly put it, "If the Spirit of God detects anything in you that is wrong, He does not ask you to put it right; He asks you to accept the light and He will put it right." [1]

The power of God's Holy Spirit enables us to remain faithful, but never compels us to do so. We maintain our free will. Just as Jonathan was forced to choose between allegiance to Saul and his covenant with David, you and I will be called upon to make choices. Each time we choose to honor our Covenant, we are symbolically clothing ourselves

---

[1] *My Utmost for His Highest* by Oswald Chambers. © 1935 by Dodd Mead & Co., renewed © 1963 by the Oswald Chambers Publications Assn., Ltd., and is used by permission of Discovery House Publishers, Box 3566, Grand Rapids, MI 49501. All rights reserved. Page 83.

in the robe of Jesus Christ, and the power of His Holy Spirit insures our success. Here are some areas in which we are called upon to make a choice:

- *Put on the Lord Jesus Christ and make no provision for the flesh in regard to its lusts* (Romans 13:14 emphasis added).

What are the lusts of our flesh? They are legitimate desires which, when over-indulged or illegitimately satisfied, become lustful, insatiable appetites. I once had a Bible teacher who called them the three G's: Glory, Gold, and Guys (or Gals as the case may be). At times we are all tempted by pride, greed, and lust, but victory is ensured when we make a conscious decision to put on the robe of our Covenant Partner. It is then that His strength undergirds us and keeps us from failing. The choice is ours.

- *Lay aside the deeds of darkness and put on the armor of light* (Romans 13:12–13 emphasis added).

The deeds of darkness are those things which are maliciously done in secret. In a broad sense, they include lying, stealing, causing dissensions, divisions, murder, and all acts of immorality. This is a very personal area, and only you know what it means in your life—that weakness which repeatedly trips you up when you least expect it. If you are in Covenant with God, you can choose to put on the robe of your Covenant Partner and receive the power to walk away from it. Again, it is a choice.

- *Put on a heart of compassion, kindness, humility, gentleness and patience, bearing with one another, forgiving each other* (Colossians 3:12–13 emphasis added).
- *Put on love, which is the perfect bond of unity* (Colossians 3:14 emphasis added).

The Greek word for *put on* is *enduo* and it means "to sink into, to go under." The indwelling of God's Holy Spirit enables Christians to "sink into" or "go under" His power, thereby exhibiting the characteristics of Jesus. When tempted to be lustful, dishonest, insensitive, judgmental, unkind, arrogant, harsh, impatient, apathetic, unforgiving, or unloving (and at times, all of us are so tempted), as God's Covenant partners, we can *choose to put on* the robe of our Covenant Partner. The moment we decide to remain faithful, His supernatural power enables us to keep Covenant with Him.

THE EXCHANGE OF WEAPONS

The exchanging of weapons between Jonathan and David symbolized their promise of mutual protection. Each was vowing to fight and to die if necessary to defend the other. The lives of Jonathan and David indicate that they both upheld this commitment. Jonathan did his part in helping David escape from Saul. After the deaths of Saul and Jonathan, when David became king, he honored his covenant with Jonathan by giving aid and protection to

A Covenant in Action

Jonathan's only living son, Mephibosheth. It was customary for a new king to execute all of the previous king's relatives; therefore, David's benevolence to Mephibosheth publicly demonstrated the sacredness of his covenant vow. He not only spared Mephibosheth, but went out of his way to find him, inquiring of his servants, *"Is there yet anyone left of the house of Saul, that I may show him kindness for Jonathan's sake?"* (2 Samuel 9:1). When he learned of Mephibosheth's whereabouts, David immediately sent this message to him: *"Do not fear, for I will surely show kindness to you for the sake of your father Jonathan, and will restore to you all the land of your grandfather, Saul; and you shall eat at my table regularly"* (2 Samuel 9:7). It is clear that both Jonathan and David understood and honored their exchange of weapons.

The question is, when we enter into Covenant with God today, does He take on our enemies? Yes, of course, He does. Here are just a few of the promises given to His Covenant partners.

- *Many are the afflictions of the righteous; but the Lord delivers him out of them all* (Psalm 34:19).
- *The Lord is faithful, and He will strengthen and protect you from the evil one* (2 Thessalonians 3:3).
- *He will cover you with His pinions, and under His wings you may seek refuge; His faithfulness is a shield and bulwark* (Psalm 91:4).
- *For He will give His angels charge concerning you, to guard you in all your ways* (Psalm 91:11).
- *The name of the Lord is a strong tower; The righteous runs into it and is safe* (Proverbs 18:10).

- *He only is my rock and my salvation, my stronghold; I shall not be greatly shaken* (Psalm 62:2).

There are times when the enemy is not a person but rather a situation that is beyond our control. Many years ago I was asked to address a women's Bible study. It was the first time I had taught a large group and I was keenly aware of the butterflies in my stomach. As the introduction concluded and I looked across the crowded sanctuary, my eyes were drawn to Sarah, a young woman seated directly in front of the podium. Looking into her face brought a knot to my stomach and plummeted me into a nightmarish flashback.

My husband I have two daughters, Tammy and Susan. When Tammy was fourteen years old, she was quite active in the church youth group, and took it upon herself to befriend a troubled sixteen year old named Sarah. Sarah was a high school dropout, and no longer lived with her parents. Tammy asked if she could stay with us. After discussing it, we decided that we would allow Sarah to stay, if she agreed to return to high school and continued to be an active part of the youth group. Sarah assured us that she would and moved in. Almost immediately, I felt uncomfortable with the relationship between Sarah and Tammy. I couldn't put my finger on what was troubling me, yet I felt very strongly that something was wrong. Silently I wrestled with these feelings, even questioning whether I could possibly be jealous of their relationship. But when the uneasiness persisted, I decided to speak with our church youth director. He listened patiently as I tried to explain feelings I did not understand. Then he apologetically informed me that he was aware of Sarah's problem with lesbianism. Well, that was ALL I needed to hear! I was certainly willing to help a troubled teenager, but I was NOT willing to place my daughters in harm's way. We mothers have much in common with enraged grizzlies when it comes to protecting our young. As far as I was concerned, Sarah was already as good as gone.

Thankfully, my husband is less impulsive and proved to be the voice of reason once again. We prayed together, asking what God would have us do in this awkward situation. Later that week, we met with Sarah and told her that we were aware of her problem, but were willing for her to remain with us if she agreed to receive Christian counseling. We were both naïve and unprepared for her, "No way, man!" response, as she stormed out of our home, slamming the door behind her. All of us were upset, but it was an especially difficult time for Tammy. She felt so certain that we were to minister to Sarah. With angry tears streaming down her cheeks, she sobbed, "God says that I should honor and obey you so I will, but I think you're wrong." I wanted to put my arms around her and try to make her understand our decision, but she was too upset. Searching for the right words, I finally heard myself confessing, "Tammy, I know you can't understand this right now, but I love you so much that I will risk losing your love to protect you." Now with flashbacks of that painful scene replaying in my mind, I looked again into Sarah's face and silently prayed, "God, please anoint what You have given me to share tonight and keep me from being distracted."

Afterwards as I was leaving the building, Sarah approached, saying that she wanted to apologize. I expected her to apologize for the way in which she had stormed out of our home, but to my surprise she said that she was sorry for having walked out in the middle of my presentation. She explained that she had become overwhelmed by conviction and emotion and had exited the sanctuary by walking down the center aisle. I managed to muddle through accepting her apology, but I felt confused. The podium had been positioned directly in front of Sarah's seat, so it would have been impossible for her to walk down the center aisle without my seeing her.

On the drive home that evening I expressed my puzzlement to God, and He reminded me that He is God of the impossible. I recalled how Peter escaped prison by walking past guards who never saw him. I remembered stories about missionaries who successfully smuggled unconcealed Bibles past border guards. I cannot explain how God did it, but I know that He answered my prayer and shielded me from what would have been an unnecessary and hurtful distraction. Proverbs 30:5 says, *"He is a shield to those who take refuge in Him."*

Here is another question which deserves our consideration. If God, as our Covenant Partner, takes on our enemies, how are we to treat them? Jesus said, *"Love your enemies, and pray for those who persecute you"* (Matthew 5:44). David understood what it meant to love his enemy. Saul chased after him with three thousand men. On one occasion, when Saul became weary, he went into a cave to sleep, unaware that David and his men were hiding in the cave. Of course, David's men wanted to kill Saul, but David prevented it saying, *"Far be it from me because of the LORD that I should do this thing to the LORD'S anointed, to stretch out my hand against him, since he is the LORD'S anointed"* (1 Samuel 24:6). Instead of killing him, David merely cut off the edge of Saul's robe. The next morning, he called to Saul, saying, *"See the edge of your robe in my hand! For in that I cut off the edge of your robe and did not kill you, know and perceive that there is no evil or rebellion in my hands, and I have not sinned against you, though you are lying in wait for my life to take it. May the LORD judge between you and me, and may the LORD avenge me on you; but my hand shall not be against you"* (1 Samuel 24:11–12).

Later, David was given another opportunity to kill Saul. Once again he refused saying, *"Who can stretch out his hand against the LORD'S anointed and be without guilt?"* (1 Samuel 26:9). David's heart is clearly seen in these two incidents. He knew that he was anointed to be king, but until the time that God inaugurated it, David regarded Saul as God's anointed, and treated him respectfully. Not lifting a finger against Saul, David left the situation entirely in God's hands.

To be honest, behaving in a kind and loving way towards those who hurt us seems impossible, and it is. Christianity is never difficult, it is absolutely impossible apart from the indwelling power of God's Holy Spirit. However, *if* we are in Covenant with God, and *if* we choose to "put on" the robe of our Covenant Partner, we can respond as David did. We can treat our enemies with respect. We can place every unpleasant situation in our Covenant Partner's hand, knowing that it will be taken care of in God's perfect timing. Here is a contemporary story, illustrating this truth.

Jennifer is a Christian and a prolific songwriter. Encouraged by her friends and family, she submitted songs to a Nashville publisher. He responded affirmatively, requested a down payment, and made plans for her to cut a demo tape in Nashville. After sending the requested money, Jennifer began hearing horror stores about charlatans in the music business. Consequently, she did a bit of inquiring and found this particular publisher to be of poor reputation. However, since she had already sent money, she had no choice but to go along with the agenda.

Thinking that she could have fallen victim to someone who made his living by exploiting the dreams of others was upsetting, and Jennifer turned to her Covenant Partner for help. "God, please cause this man to be honest in all his dealings with me," she prayed, day in and day out, as the trip to Nashville approached. Then one morning, God directed her attention to Psalm 18:26: "*With the pure Thou dost show Thyself pure; and with the crooked Thou dost show Thyself astute.*" It was just one little line and yet it spoke volumes to her heart, confirming what she already knew to be true. She need not worry, because her Covenant Partner was well aware of the situation and would show Himself to be more clever than Mr. Nashville Publisher.

With a warning flag waving in her heart, Jennifer flew to Nashville, recorded a demo with talented musicians, and was Mr. Publisher's dinner guest that evening. He promised to have the demo tape delivered to her within four weeks which, of course, did not happen. Every day for months Jennifer prayed, "God, show Yourself as astute to this man," as he continued to lie, stall, and prove himself to be an unscrupulous character. Yet through it all, Jennifer continued trusting her Covenant Partner. Finally, Mr. Publisher showed up on Jennifer's doorstep to deliver what would be his last excuse. Claiming that his wife was dying of cancer, he sought Jennifer's sympathy and a further extension of time. Appearing to believe him and seizing the moment, Jennifer insisted, "Let me pray with you." Taking hold of his hand, she prayed, asking that God extend His mercy and healing to Mrs. Publisher. As she whispered "Amen" and opened her eyes, Jennifer was surprised to see Mr. Publisher's scarlet face and trembling hands. She took a step forward, intending to give him a hug, but he lunged for the door, making a hasty, awkward exit. A few days later, Jennifer received her demo tape and all that had been promised to her. Obviously, she learned an important lesson regarding the music industry, but certainly it was also a learning experience for Mr. Publisher. He discovered that he could not cheat one of God's Covenant partners and get away with it. *"Though they intended evil against Thee, and devised a plot, they will not succeed"* (Psalm 21:11). Yes indeed! We have a Covenant Partner who does take on our enemies.

Since we are in a covenant relationship, aren't we required to take on God's enemies as well? Yes, of course, we are. Who is His enemy and how do we fight? Obviously, Satan remains God's archenemy. His utmost desire is to keep individuals ignorant of God's Covenant plan. In the Garden of Eden, he told Eve that she did not need God because she could eat the forbidden fruit and become like God. He continues to sing that same old song today. Updating it with a New Age twist, he adds "You *are* god. Your higher self is divine. You just have to get in touch with it." This melodious lie can be heard resonating from New Age book shelves, and reaching a screeching crescendo in the religious sections. So how do we fight? In answer, permit me to borrow a phrase from Terry Brooks, one of my favorite Bible teachers. "Don't attack the darkness, turn on the light." Light always dispels darkness. In other words, allowing others to see the love and peace of God lived out in our lives is detrimental to Satan's scheme. Christians are not exempt from pain and sorrow. In fact, Jesus prepared believers for hardship when He said, *"In the world you have tribulation, but take courage; I have overcome the world"* (John 16:33). When others see that we have peace and hope in the midst of difficult circumstances, we are turning on a light. We are allowing them to witness the light of God's kingdom, overpowering the darkness of the world. In writing to believers in Ephesus, Paul wrote, *"For you were formerly darkness, but now you are light in the Lord; walk as children of light"* (Ephesians 5:9). And John was writing in the same vein when he penned these words to fellow believers, *"If we walk in the light as He Himself is in the light, we have fellowship with one another"* (1 John 1:7). Unbelievers recognize the true light emanating from someone who is walking with God, someone who has peace in the midst of chaos, and someone who loves fellow believers regardless of their denominational differences because of the Holy Spirit within them. It is God's Covenant in action, and it strikes an effective blow against God's archenemy.

Another formidable weapon which Christians are privileged to launch against God's enemy is prayer. Satan can do nothing to stop an individual from praying. Any time and in any place, we are free to communicate with our Covenant Partner—praying for others, for cities, for nations, or even for ourselves. If we do not know how to pray for a particular situation, we ask and God's Holy Spirit directs us. *"The Spirit helps our weakness; for we do not know how to pray as we should, but the Spirit Himself intercedes for us with groanings too deep for words, and He who searches the hearts knows what the mind of the Spirit is, because He intercedes for the saints according to the will of God"* (Romans 8:26–27). Nothing can prevent prayer. Laws cannot stop it, threats cannot weaken it, prisons cannot restrain it, and spiritual forces cannot withstand it. Prayer is divinely given and supernaturally executed. Nothing can hinder this powerful weapon!

One more offensive, as well as defensive, weapon that foils Satan's most elaborate plan is having knowledge of God's Word. Second Timothy 2:15 says, *"Be diligent to present yourself approved to God, as a workman who does not need to be ashamed, handling accurately the word of truth."* Getting to know God's Word takes time. Our new heart and God's Holy Spirit initiate the desire, but we must take the time to study. When I first began reading my Bible every day, I would set the timer on my stove for five minutes. Being a busy mother of two, it was all the time I felt I could spare. I soon discovered that the Holy Spirit used those five minutes a day to teach me how to effectively defeat God's enemy. When Jesus was tempted in the wilderness, He defeated Satan by using the Word of God. It still works for His Covenant partners today.

THE EXCHANGING OF ARMOR AND BELTS

The exchanging of armor and belts symbolized an exchange of strength between Jonathan and David. The belt, also called a girdle, was not a dinky, designer original. It was a wide, leather strap that protected a man's abdomen, his lower back, and held his weapons in place. When the belt was worn properly, the armor was in place, a soldier's weapons were easily accessible, his vital organs covered, and he was the personification of power. First Samuel 23:16 says that Jonathan *"arose and went to David at Horesh, and encouraged him in God."* Another translation says that *"he strengthened his hand."* Jonathan gave strength to David in the form of reassurance. He said to him, *"Do not be afraid, because the hand of Saul, my father, shall not find you, and you will be king over Israel and I will be next to you; and Saul, my father, knows that also"* (1 Samuel 23:17). Until David became King, he spent his days running from Saul. During those years, it was Jonathan who did the strengthening. However, after Jonathan's death, when David became king, he honored his covenant by lending his strength to Jonathan's crippled son, Mephibosheth. Not only did David restore all of Saul's land to Mephibosheth, but he also enlisted forty-two servants to work the land, since Mephibosheth's handicap prevented his doing so. David honored his covenant with Jonathan by treating Mephibosheth as if he were one of his own sons, sharing all he possessed with him, and thus enabling him to live a productive life.

A Covenant in Action

Since a covenant relationship demands that the partners lend their strength to each other, God promised to give His strength to those who belong to Him.

- *He gives strength to the weary; and to him who lacks might, He increases power (Isaiah 40:29).*
- *The salvation of the righteous is from the Lord; He is their strength in time of trouble (Psalm 37:39).*

The following promise from Isaiah 40:31 makes it perfectly clear that God takes the human weakness of His Covenant partners and replaces it with His strength.

Those who wait for the LORD will gain new strength They will mount up with wings like eagles, They will run and not get tired, They will walk and not become weary.

The Hebrew word *wait* used in this passage is *qawah* and it means, "to bind together or to be joined." The Hebrew word for *gain* is *chalaph* and it means, "to change, or to pass on." God is saying that those who are joined to Him (meaning those who are in Covenant with Him), will have their strength changed or exchanged for His strength. The apostle Paul attempted to explain this exchange of strength to the Corinthians when he wrote, *"And He [God] said to me, 'My grace is sufficient for you, for power is perfected in weakness'. I will rather boast about my weaknesses, that the power of Christ may dwell in me. Therefore I am well content with weakness, with insults, with distresses, with persecutions, with difficulties, for Christ's sake; for when I am weak, then I am strong"* (2 Corinthians 12:9–10). The Greek word translated *power* in 2 Corinthians

12:9–10 is *dunamis* and it refers to God's miracle-working power. Paul was proclaiming that when he reached the end of his own strength, his Covenant Partner took over and strengthened him. Paul boldly declared, *"I can do all things through Him who strengthens me"* (Philippians 4:13). We can almost hear the thundering voice of Oswald Chambers echoing in agreement: *"It is a positive crime to be weak in God's strength."*[2] There are times when Christians become weary, and sad, but they need never be weak. God's Covenant promises that Christians may depend upon the Lord to meet them at the point of their weakness and to fill them with His strength, whether it is emotional, mental, physical, or spiritual. Later, we will see how God gave strength to men during biblical times, but here is a contemporary example of God's infusion of strength to one of His Covenant partners.

In 1975 Beau was an avid racquetball player, participating in many tournaments. One in particular will always stand out in his mind as the day he discovered the practicality of God's Covenant. There were no age brackets in this particular tournament, and thirty-five-year-old Beau found himself competing against youngsters barely in their twenties. It proved to be physically grueling and by the end of the second day, Beau was well aware of his years. Whenever a time out was called, he collapsed in a corner, wiped the stinging sweat from his eyes, and prayed for the strength to continue. Each time, he got up feeling energized, and the cycle of fa-

---

[2] *My Utmost for His Highest* by Oswald Chambers. © 1935 by Dodd Mead & Co., renewed © 1963 by the Oswald Chambers Publications Assn., Ltd., and is used by permission of Discovery House Publishers, Box 3566, Grand Rapids, MI 49501. All rights reserved. Page 105.

A Covenant in Action

tigue, prayer, and strength took him through the remainder of the tournament. At the close of the third day, dripping with perspiration and visibly exhausted, Beau was awarded the first-place trophy. Friends and family celebrated his victory, but Beau knew that an even greater victory had been won spiritually. He would always remember this tournament as the first time he experienced God's willingness to exchange human weakness for His divine strength in a very ordinary way. God will do the same for you and me. It is simply a part of being in Covenant with Him.

Since Christianity is a Covenant relationship, we are expected to give God our strength. How do we do that? Surrendering our strength to God is perhaps more difficult than giving Him our weakness, because it involves our pride. God warns us about the dangers of pride in His Word, saying, *"Pride goes before destruction, and a haughty spirit before stumbling"* and *"A man's pride will bring him low"* (Proverbs 16:18, 29:23). To operate in pride is "the deification of self." [3] It is denying the fact that we have a Covenant Partner, and to those who are tempted to do so, God gives this warning in 1 Corinthians 10:12: *"Let him who thinks he stands take heed lest he fall."* The great men of the Bible fell on their strong points, never on their weak ones. Finding themselves to be outnumbered or overpowered, they readily sought God's help. It was only when they thought themselves adequate for the task at hand and attempted it alone, that they failed. We are much the same.

---

[3] *My Utmost for His Highest* by Oswald Chambers, @1935 by Dodd Mead & Co., renewed @ 1963 by the Oswald Chambers Publications Assn., Ltd., and is used by permission of Discovery House Publishers, Box 3566, Grand Rapids, MI 49501. All rights reserved. Page 164.

Finding ourselves at our wits' end, we readily acknowledge our need of God. However, when we are feeling strong and self-reliant, we behave like children refusing parental assistance. "I can do it by myself," we indignantly insist. Then we fail. Blinded by inflated egos, we cannot see that a powerful, conniving, deceitful enemy lurks in the shadows, ready to take us down at any moment. Doing anything without our Covenant Partner's involvement is sheer foolishness. You may be thinking that God doesn't want to be bothered by the trivial things in your life, assuming that it is immature to rely on Him so completely. To the contrary, it is a sign of spiritual maturity. When you understand a covenant relationship, you realize that God is honored when you surrender your strengths as well as your weaknesses to Him. I recently saw a church marquee that stated it like this: "If God is your co-pilot, change seats."

Looking at the covenant between Jonathan and David shows that a covenant promises unity, strength, and protection to the individuals involved. It is a sacred bond, requiring the commitment of both parties. It is stronger than family ties, greater than personal ambition, and takes precedence over every area of life. In addition, God's Covenant is eternal. A young man once boasted that he was born a Christian. That might be possible if Christianity were a religion, but God calls it a Covenant. This means that every individual must personally choose to enter or reject this Covenant relationship with God. There is no middle ground. We are either in or out. We may have been born into a Christian home, and persuaded by parents to follow Christian principles, but being a Christian means that we have made a conscious decision to enter into Covenant with God through Jesus Christ.

A Covenant in Action

Further understanding of God's Covenant requires that we look closely at the Old Testament. Since God said that He does not change, what we see pictured in the lives of these Old Testament believers becomes vital to our understanding of Covenant today. Concerning these Old Testament happenings, Paul wrote, *"these things happened to them as an example, and they were written for our instruction, upon whom the ends of the ages have come"* (1 Corinthians 10:11). God knew how difficult it would be for us to grasp His concept of Covenant; therefore, He made certain that it was carefully recorded and pictured in His word over and over again. Afterwards, He probably smiled as He promised, *"You will seek Me and find Me when you search for Me with all your heart"* (Jeremiah 29:13). Finding God and entering into Covenant with Him is a journey of the heart. When we strip away our religious masks and seek God with all our hearts, He promises that we will find Him. We will know the joy of a daily, eternal Covenant relationship with the King of kings and LORD of Lords.

On the following page is a genealogy chart which traces God's Covenant promise from its origin in the Garden of Eden to its fulfillment in Jesus Christ. Sixty-six generations span the years between Adam and Jesus. And although space prohibits all of these being listed, using the chart as an outline we are going to travel through the Old Testament, stopping along the way to look more closely at the lives of just a few of the individuals who were chosen to carry God's Covenant message to their generations. In doing so, we will be viewing the Covenant from different perspectives, seeing it operate in various situations, and thereby gaining greater insight into our own Covenant relationship with God.

The Forgotten Covenant

Abridged Genealogy Chart

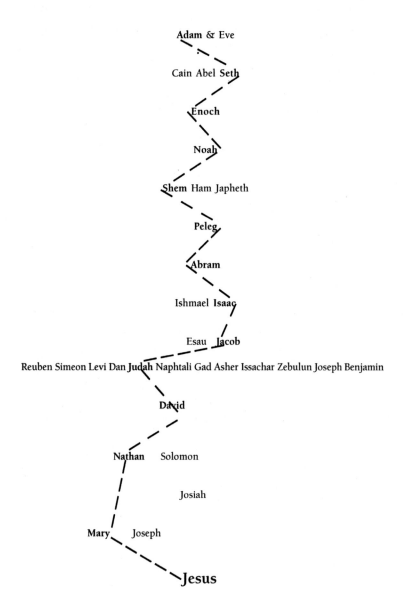

Chapter 3

THE BEGINNING OF GOD'S COVENANT

(Adam and Eve)

God's Covenant began with Adam and Eve in a garden called Eden. The story of creation is a familiar one, recorded in the first chapters of the book of Genesis. We are told that God created the earth, the animals, man, and woman, and they all lived harmoniously together, until the day that Adam and Eve ate from the forbidden tree.

Their disobedience not only changed their lives, but it altered the lives of all who were to come after them. Because they violated God's command, they were removed from the garden, relocated in a strange land, and experienced hardship for the first time in their lives. Eve, who had never encountered so much as hangnail, underwent a crash course in pain called "Childbirth 101." Adam, who was accustomed to leisurely partaking of the most exquisite edibles in the garden, now found himself thrust into the role of provider. Waging war against weeds, thorns, insects, and hungry animals, he tilled, planted, and harvested crops. Adam and Eve proved to be quite resourceful in adapting to their new environment, and in time scarcely resembled their former selves. Exposure to the elements etched its telltale lines across their weather-beaten faces. Joints ached, eyes dimmed, hearing diminished, and hair turned gray as they journeyed ever closer to becoming inevitable piles of dust. All of this is what they received because of their disobedience, but more importantly, what had they lost? What was the most precious possession Adam and Eve lost when they disobeyed God? Answering this question requires that we look at their lives prior to the fall.

Genesis chapters 1, 2, and 3 give us a glimpse of the life Adam and Eve lived in the Garden of Eden. We are told that God walked with them and talked with them in the garden. Nowhere in those beginning chapters do we see Adam and Eve doing anything that could be termed religious. There were no altars, no fasting, and no mandatory prayers. Adam and Eve were not religious fanatics. They were simply a man and woman enjoying an intimate, loving relationship with their God. He was their Father, and as His children, they basked in the joy of sharing their lives with Him. Unfortunately, when they disobeyed, they became separated from God. Among other things, this meant that they could no longer remain in the garden, although they were free to live anywhere they chose in the new land. They no longer had access to the abundance of food in the garden, but if they worked diligently, the new land would yield sufficient crops to feed them. There was also an ample supply of raw materials to be used for shelter and clothing.

The Beginning of God's Covenant

They lacked only one irreplaceable thing—God's presence. In forfeiting their personal relationship with Him, they lost their most precious possession.

Have you ever wondered what it was like for Adam and Eve to walk and talk with God in the Garden of Eden? How must it have felt to know that every day would be perfect—no storms, no earthquakes, no terrorists, no wars, no sickness, no disharmony of any kind? Adam and Eve were the only human beings to know absolute peace and unconditional love as a way of life. They enjoyed the environment God intended for all of us. Today, in this twenty-first century, it is practically impossible to imagine that kind of stress-free existence. It seems that everyone, regardless of age, suffers from some form of stress. Yet, somewhere in the deepest resources of our being there remains a faint recollection of what used to be. Somehow we know that once upon a time things were very different, and knowing that gives rise to a longing within us. We long for peace. We long to be loved unconditionally, and we long to feel connected to something beyond ourselves. For the most part, the still small voice of this longing is easily lost amid the clamor of our busy, everyday lives. But every now and then, when we find ourselves captivated by the incredible splendor of a sunset, or mesmerized by a star-studded mountain top sky, we hear that familiar, hushed voice from within, affirming anew what we know in our hearts to be true. We were created to be a part of something eternal. We were created to experience the love and the peace that Adam and Eve once knew. We were created to walk with God.

Walking and talking with God was so much a part of Adam and Eve's everyday life that they most likely took it for granted, until the day that Satan enticed Eve and upset paradise. Scripture tells us that *"the serpent was more crafty than any beast of the field which the LORD God had made. And he said to the woman, 'Indeed has God said, "You shall not eat from any tree of the garden?"'* (Genesis 3:1). Satan asked what appeared to be an innocent question, but his motive was deadly. Well aware of God's instructions concerning the forbidden tree, he planned to lure Eve into betrayal. In answering his question, Eve replied, *"From the fruit of the trees of the garden we may eat; but from the fruit of the tree which is in the middle of the garden, God has said, 'You shall not eat from it or touch it, lest you die.'"* (Genesis 3:3). Unintentionally, Eve had taken the bait. Satan must have been scarcely able to conceal his delight as he set the hook. *"You surely shall not die!"* he mocked. *"For God knows that in the day you eat from it your eyes will be opened, and you will be like God, knowing good and evil"* (Genesis 3:4–5).

His words fell upon Eve like a ton of bricks. Feeling shocked and confused, she wondered, *"Could Satan be telling the truth? Is God selfishly withholding this blessing from us?"* In her bewilderment Eve unconsciously inched nearer the tree. As she did, she *"saw that the tree was good for food, and that it was a delight to the eyes, and that the tree was desirable to make one wise"* (Genesis 3:6). Cognizant of her confusion, Satan continued coaxing, "Go ahead, try it. You surely shall not die. Taste it! You will become like God." Within an arm's reach of the tree, Satan's chant became a hypnotic dirge, reverberating in her mind, *"You surely shall not die. You will be like God. You surely shall not die. You will be like God!"* Louder and louder it echoed, as her hand slowly reached toward the fruit. Perhaps she even dared to allow a finger to tentatively brush against it. And NOTHING HAPPENED! There were no lightning bolts, no thunderous rebuttal from heaven, and she certainly did not drop dead. Satan must be telling the truth, Eve concluded. So *"she took from its fruit and ate; and she gave also to her husband with her, and he ate"* (Genesis 3:6).

Looking at these verses gives insight into the tactics of the enemy. Satan is a cowardly, crafty and merciless master of deception. Asking what appeared to be a harmless question, he seduced Eve into conversation. Eve, being ignorant of the danger involved in conversing with God's enemy, fell victim to his diabolical scheme. Unfortunately, when we are ignorant of Satan's tactics, we too can become a victim.

When we are feeling insecure, Satan tries to imprison us with painful reminders of past failures. When we are afraid, he attempts to paralyze us with incessant "What if" questions—What if this happens? What if that happens? What if God doesn't care, or what if God is punishing you?—until all hope is lost in a sea of tragic possibilities. When we are hurt, sick, or lonely, he offers us a sip from his poisonous cup of self-pity, and we ingest his vicious lie: "God doesn't care about you." If we fail, he mockingly chides, "God will never forgive you." Being an evil, sadistic coward, he is swift to take advantage of any situation that weakens us physically, emotionally, or spiritually, in the hope of getting us to doubt God's love, His character, and our relationship with Him, just as he did with Eve. But the good news is that Satan is no match for our Covenant Partner, who gives us strength and weapons to use against such attacks.

Knowing that our mind is the battlefield and that conversations with Satan are deadly, God provided a weapon, which is found in 2 Corinthians 10:5: *"Take every thought captive to the obedience of Christ."* What does that mean? How do we do it? It means that because Satan is able to place thoughts into our minds, God instructs us to take every troubling thought and pass it through a filter which He has provided for this very purpose. The filter is found in Philippians 4:8: "Finally, *brethren, whatever is true, whatever is honorable, whatever is right, whatever is pure, whatever is lovely, whatever is of good repute, if there is any excellence and if anything worthy of praise, let your mind dwell on these things."* When a disturbing thought enters our mind, we are to first ask ourselves if it is true. Since Satan is a liar, it will very often be a lie. If it is a lie, we reject the thought, telling him that God has instructed us to dwell on the things which are true. If it happens to be true, we simply move on to the next grid, asking if it is honorable. If so, we move on to the next and on to the next, until the thought gets caught in God's grid. When it does, we inform Satan that the thought is contrary to God's Word, and we therefore reject it. This will silence him, as illustrated in the following example of one young woman's victory over such attacks.

Madeline left the doctor's office choking back tears. She scarcely reached the privacy of her car before convulsing in anguished sobs. The doctor's words, "If you make it to twenty-six weeks, we will hospitalize you," felt like a knife piercing her heart. Madeline wanted this baby more than anything else in the world.

After months of trying, the test had finally read positive, and she and Gil could not wait to tell their families.

The Beginning of God's Covenant

Everything was wonderful. Even the morning sickness seemed a small price to pay for such incredible joy. A setback occurred when the pregnancy was diagnosed as high risk, and Madeline was placed on bed rest. It was an adjustment to be sure, but Madeline quit her job, and Gil managed to do most of the housework. Together they made certain that she followed the doctor's orders to a "T", which now only added to the frustration she felt. This new development was beyond anyone's control. There was nothing that she or the doctor could do, and if what he suspected turned out to be true, there was little chance that she would carry the baby to twenty-six weeks.

"God, please don't let me lose this baby," she pleaded. Instantly, she heard a familiar voice speaking in her mind. "You don't deserve this baby. You aborted a child when you were seventeen, and now you have the audacity to ask God to help you carry this one. I don't think so!" Subconsciously responding, Madeline shook her head in agreement. "You're right," she admitted. "I did have an abortion when I was seventeen. I don't deserve God's help now." No sooner had the thought entered her mind, than the Holy Spirit came to her defense, giving Madeline the wisdom and strength to fight.

She had recently become a Christian, and since her condition prevented her from attending a Bible Study, Madeline received weekly cassette tapes of the lesson. It was something she remembered hearing on a tape that now came to mind, a scripture from Ephesians: *"Be strong in the Lord and in the strength of His might. Put on the full armor of God that you may be able to stand firm against the schemes of the devil. For our struggle is not against flesh and blood, but against the rulers, against the powers, against the world forces of this darkness, against the spiritual forces of wickedness in the heavenly places"* (6:10–12). Realizing that she was experiencing a full-blown attack from the enemy of her soul, Madeline prayed, asking for God's help.

Immediately the Holy Spirit reminded her of the weapon she was to use. *"Take every thought captive to the obedience of Christ"* (2 Corinthians 10:5). So taking the awful thought captive, Madeline passed it through the first grid, asking herself, "Is what I am hearing true?" Yes, she had to admit that it was true. Moving quickly on to the next grid, she asked, "Is it honorable?" The answer was a resounding, "No"! It certainly did not honor her, but worst of all, it slandered God's character. As a new Christian, she had much to learn; yet, she knew enough to be certain that God was not sitting up in heaven waiting for an opportunity to punish her. She knew that He loved her and had forgiven her. The Holy Spirit was quick to remind her of that assurance given in 1 John 1:9: *"If we confess our sins, He is faithful and righteous to forgive us our sins and to cleanse us from all unrighteousness."* She also remembered that somewhere in the Bible it says that God removes our transgressions *"as far as the east is from the west"* and that *"He remembers them no more"* (Psalm 103:12, Isaiah 43:25).

Strengthened by the power of her Covenant Partner and determined not to entertain any more lies, Madeline fought hard. With tears streaming down her cheeks, she drove home that afternoon, quoting as many Scriptures as she could to remind herself of God's love and protection. As she did, the enemy's voice was silenced. Her physical condition was serious, and the pregnancy beyond her control; nevertheless she felt comforted by the fact that, she was choosing to place herself and her baby in God's loving hands.

In the weeks that followed, Madeline endured many more encounters with the enemy. Without warning, a condemning or fearful thought would pop into her mind. Each time it did, she forced herself to sift it through God's Philippians 4:8 grid. Time after time, she rejected the lies, spoke God's Word, and silenced the enemy of her soul. It was an emotionally draining, laborious fight, but as she faithfully wielded this powerful weapon, the attacks became less frequent and stopped during the ninth month.

Words could not express their joy and thankfulness when Madeline and Gil became the proud parents of a beautiful baby girl. They knew that laying peacefully within their arms was a miracle. As Madeline tenderly rocked her sleeping infant, she reflected upon the struggles of the previous nine months, and silently vowed to teach her precious daughter about God's love and His Covenant. She determined that her child would know how to *"take every thought captive to the obedience of Christ"* at an early age.

Jesus called Satan *"the father of lies"* (John 8:44). Being true to his nature, Satan lied when he spoke to Eve. Attempting to malign God's character, he insinuated that God was deliberately and selfishly withholding a blessing from them. Then betting the success of his entire plan on the assumption that Eve had no understanding of spiritual death, Satan blatantly denied God's word, saying, *"You surely shall not die!"* (Genesis 3:4). That was a lie. He knew that she would not instantly drop dead, but that the process of physical death would be set into motion and more importantly, spiritual separation from God would be instantaneous. Satan lied to Eve in the garden and he lies to us today, still attempting to cast doubt on God's character and His love for us, just as he did with Eve.

If you are searching for a relationship with God, the chances are good that Satan will lie to you as you read this book. He may remind you of a past that you wish could be forgotten. He may tell you that God could never love nor forgive you. He might say that it's too late for you; you've gone too far. He may imply that God is punishing you, as he did with Madeline. That would be in keeping with his character because he is the father of lies. The truth is that *"neither death, nor life, nor angels, nor principalities, nor things present, nor things to come, nor powers, nor height, nor depth, nor any other created thing shall be able to separate us from the love of God which is in Christ Jesus our Lord"* (Romans 8:38–39). And Jesus lovingly adds, *"The one who comes to Me I will certainly not cast out"* (John 6:37). Nothing that you or I have done can disqualify us from entering into Covenant with God, because we do not come to Him on our own merit. We come, acknowledging the fact that we have no right to walk with Him. We come because Jesus paid the price for our sins, fulfilling God's Covenant, and offering restoration of the relationship to us. If Satan speaks lies to the contrary, quote Romans 8:38–39 and John 6:37 to silence him. Absolutely nothing can separate you from the love of God, and no one who comes to Jesus is ever refused. This is the truth and it brings to mind another weapon God has given us.

This weapon is His Word. Obviously, Eve did not know the word of God for herself. Prior to the creation of Eve, God said to Adam, *"From any tree in the garden you may eat*

The Beginning of God's Covenant

freely; but from the tree of the knowledge of good and evil you shall not eat, for in the day that you eat from it, you shall surely die" (Genesis 2:16–17). However, when Eve answered Satan's question, she misquoted God's instructions, saying, *"God said, 'You shall not eat from it or touch it, lest you die'"* (Genesis 3:3). Do you see her mistake? Did God say anything about touching the tree? No, He did not. He only forbid their eating from it. This seems like a harmless mistake, but it became the catalyst for catastrophe. Permit me to suggest that because Eve did not know God's word for herself, the moment she dared to let her finger tentatively brush against the apple and nothing happened, Satan had the victory. In an instant, she came to doubt God's love and character, and believe Satan's lie. Had she known God's word for herself, things could have turned out differently.

So who is to blame for Eve's ignorance? Did Adam misquote God when he spoke to Eve regarding the tree? Perhaps afraid that curiosity might get the best of her, he added to God's instructions by telling her that she would die if she so much as touched it. Did Eve know, but just get confused in the presence of such evil? Who can say? But it does illustrate the importance of our knowing God's Word for ourselves and living our lives in accordance with it. Paul said, *"Be diligent to present yourself approved to God as a workman who does not need to be ashamed, handling accurately the word of truth"* (2 Timothy 2:15).

That day in the garden Eve was contending with only one voice, but today there are many voices calling God's love and character into question. Perhaps you have come across some in the New Age books. Claiming to be channels through which God is writing, these authors distort the truth. By taking Scriptures out of context, tweaking a word here, or adding a word or two there, just as Eve did, God's Word is misquoted and His message changed. If an individual does not know God's Word for himself, the distortion is appealing. After all, Satan is not a fool. He is the same crafty master of deception who conversed with Eve, therefore his counterfeit will always be alluring.

Denying God, Satan's humanistic message promises perfection through human effort alone. This naturally appeals to our human ego, and should have a familiar ring since it is exactly what he told Eve: *"You will be like God."* The only protection against this deception is to know God's Word for ourselves. The psalmist said, *"Thy word I have treasured in my heart, that I may not sin against Thee"* (Psalm 119:11). Eve could have withstood the temptation had she known God's word for herself, and the same can be said for you and me.

Although Adam and Eve betrayed God and lost their relationship with Him, God demonstrated His love by immediately implementing a plan to restore it. If you are a parent, permit me to put this into perspective. Imagine that your children have been kidnapped. What would you be willing to do to save them? Would you sacrifice all that you have, including your life? Of course you would, and that is exactly what God did. There in the garden, addressing Satan, God promised a Savior who would come from the seed of Eve. This Savior would strike a death blow to Satan's kingdom and offer restoration of the relationship to all who choose to once again know and walk with Him. Although the word *covenant* is not used in this particular verse, God's

The Beginning of God's Covenant

promise of a coming Savior marked the beginning of His Covenant chain, a chain that stretches link by link from Genesis through Revelation, binding the entire Word of God together and demonstrating that everything God does is related to His Covenant. Disobedience severed the relationship, but God's Covenant restores it to all who choose to come to Him.

After promising a coming Savior, God did something else for Adam and Eve. We are told that He *"made garments of skin for Adam and his wife, and clothed them"* (Genesis 3:21). Have you ever wondered why God chose animal skins? Why didn't He weave grass, sew leaves together, or shear a sheep? Why was it necessary to shed the blood of innocent animals? The answer is again linked to His Covenant. God was symbolically illustrating what had to be done to restore the lost relationship. The nakedness of Adam and Eve was visible evidence of their separation from God. Therefore, God shed the blood of an innocent animal, using its skin to provide a temporary covering for them. Someday, the innocent blood of His Son would permanently remove sin from all who would choose to enter into Covenant with Him. Until that appointed time, men would seek God's forgiveness through the shed blood of innocent animals. It was a visual depiction of the forthcoming Covenant fulfillment.

After clothing them, God removed Adam and Eve from the garden. Shortly thereafter, they began to have children. They named their first son Cain and their second son Abel. Cain, being the firstborn, should have been the one to carry on God's Covenant bloodline, but in a jealous rage, he killed his brother and God removed him from being a part of the Covenant chain. Cain was angry because God rejected his offering of fruit, while accepting Abel's animal sacrifice. Looking at this situation from the perspective of God's Covenant, we understand why the fruit was unacceptable. Since there was no blood involved in Cain's offering, it did not symbolically represent the coming Covenant fulfillment. Genesis 5:4 tells us that Adam and Eve had other sons and daughters, and a son named Seth was chosen by God to carry on His Covenant promise. Seth's genealogy is the first one recorded in Scripture for Adam's descendants because he was the first link in God's Covenant chain (Genesis 5).

Adam was one hundred thirty years old when Seth was born and he lived a total of nine hundred and thirty years. By using the information recorded in Genesis 5 and doing a bit of simple math, we discover that Adam lived to see eight generations of his descendants.

> Adam was 130 years old when his son, Seth was born. He was 235 years old when his grandson, Enosh was born.
>
> He was 325 years old when his great-grandson, Kenan was born.
>
> He was 395 years old when his great-great-grandson, Mahalalel was born.
>
> He was 460 years old when his great-great-great-grandson, Jared was born.

The Beginning of God's Covenant

He was 622 years old when his great-great-great-great-grandson, Enoch was born.

He was 687 years old when his great-great-great-great-great-grandson, Methuselah was born.

He was 874 years old when his great-great-great-great-great-great-grandson Lamach was born.

Why is this important? It is important because it tells us that for eight hundred years, Adam had opportunities to tell his descendants about the Garden of Eden, and God's promise of a coming messiah. They must have sensed a lump in his throat as he sought for words to describe the magnificence of the garden. Surely tears welled up in his eyes as he recounted the incredible joy of daily walking and talking with God. Perhaps even as they listened and watched, the longing within their own hearts witnessed to the truth of Adam's words, and they embraced the hope of one day being able to know and walk with God.

Chapter 4

A COVENANT PARTNER

Enoch

One individual who apparently embraced Adam's message of hope was his great, great, great, great-grandson, Enoch. Enoch was born when Adam was six hundred and twenty-two years old, and although we know very little about him, we are given three significant facts which distinguish him from other men.

Fact Number One: Enoch walked with God. Genesis 5:22 says, *"Enoch walked with God three hundred years after he became the father of Methuselah, and he had other sons and daughters."* Genesis 5:24 repeats, *"Enoch walked with God."* Enoch has the distinction of being the first individual outside the Garden of Eden to be described as walking with God.

Fact Number Two: Enoch was a prophet. *"Enoch in the seventh generation from Adam, prophesied, saying, 'Behold the Lord came with many thousands of His holy ones, to execute judgment upon all, and to convict all the ungodly of all their ungodly deeds which they have done in an ungodly way, and of all the harsh things which ungodly sinners have spoken against Him'"* (Jude 14–15). Notice that the word "ungodly" is used four times in this prophecy. When reading scripture, it is beneficial to notice repeated words or phrases, as they give insight into the reason these words are being spoken or written. Obviously, not everyone embraced Adam's message of hope, and Enoch was warning them of God's coming judgment.

Fact Number Three: Enoch never died. Genesis 5:23–24 tells us that *"all the days of Enoch were three hundred and sixty-five years. And Enoch walked with God and he was not, for God took him."* Enoch is one of only two individuals who never experienced physical death. The other was a prophet named Elijah, and 2 Kings 2:11 says this about him: *"Then it came about as they were going along and talking, that behold, there appeared a chariot of fire and horses of fire which separated the two of them. And Elijah went up by a whirlwind to heaven."*

Enoch walked with God, he was a prophet, and he was taken to heaven without passing through physical death. God's word says that *"it is appointed for men to die once and after this comes judgment"* (Hebrews 9:27), and since neither Enoch nor Elijah experienced physical death, some believe that they will return to earth during the tribulation period as the two witnesses spoken of in Revelation 11. They will prophesy for three and a half years, be killed by the antichrist, and God will raise them from the dead and lift them into heaven on a cloud as their enemies watch (Rev. 7–11). Since God's Word does not identify these two witnesses, it is merely a supposition; only time will tell.

Chapter  5

THE COVENANT PRESERVED

(Noah)

One of the most famous links in God's Covenant chain was Noah, born one hundred and twenty-six years after the death of Adam. If Adam's message kindled a flame of hope in the hearts of his listeners, it didn't last, for during the time of Noah, men turned their backs upon God. Forgetting about His Covenant, they indulged in every form of wickedness, and God's response was severe. *"The Lord said 'I will blot out man whom I have created from the face of the land, from man to animals to creeping things and to birds of the sky; for I am sorry that I have made them'"* (Genesis 6:7). *"But Noah found favor in the eyes of the Lord"* (Genesis 6:8). We have to stop at this point and ask how Noah found favor with God. What distinguished him from the other men of his day? Genesis 6:9 tells us that Noah was favored because *"he was a righteous man, blameless in his time; Noah walked with God."* Like Enoch, and

Adam and Eve before their disobedience, Noah walked with God. Somehow in the midst of an evil society, Noah managed to maintain a personal relationship with God, a relationship that warrants our taking a closer look.

When you hear the name Noah, what comes to mind? Contemporary drawings depict a bearded, elderly man leaning on his staff, watching animals of every size and description miraculously pair off and climb aboard a medium-sized boat. Noah was five hundred years old when God instructed him to build the ark, but since he lived to be nine hundred and fifty, he was merely middle-aged and well equipped physically and mentally for the task assigned him. Likewise, contemporary art fails to accurately convey the size of the ark. Surprisingly, it was seventy-five feet wide, forty-five feet high, and four hundred and fifty feet in length, making it one hundred and fifty feet longer than a football field. Its overall dimensions made it not only seaworthy, but comparable to that of modern-day ships.

A construction site of that size most likely attracted a great deal of attention, and since Noah lived in a wicked society, we have to wonder how he kept the ark from being vandalized. Did he hire guards, or did God's angels supernaturally protect it? We know that Noah lived in the desert and was therefore probably not a ship builder by trade. So how did he manage to build this enormous boat? Did he hire professionals? Did God just give him supernatural wisdom? Did his sons assist him? There are many questions which cannot be answered, yet there is much we can learn from this man called Noah.

After giving Noah careful instructions regarding the design and construction of the ark, God used the word covenant for the first time. He said, "*I will establish My covenant with you; and you shall enter the ark—you and your sons and your wife, and your sons' wives with you*" (Genesis 6:18). After the flood waters receded, God mentioned this covenant a second time. He said, "*Now behold, I Myself do establish My covenant with you, and with your descendants after you; and with every living creature that is with you . . . And I establish My covenant with you; and all flesh shall never again be cut off by the water of the flood, neither shall there again be a flood to destroy the earth*" (Genesis 9:9–11). Notice that God *established* this covenant with Noah. He did not cut it. Therefore, there was no blood involved. God simply gave this covenant as an unconditional, everlasting gift to all generations. To help us remember, He gave a sign. He said, "*I set My bow in the cloud, and it shall be for a sign of a covenant between Me and the earth*" (Genesis 9:13). "*When the bow is in the cloud then I will look upon it, to remember the everlasting covenant between God and every living creature of all flesh that is on the earth*" (Genesis 9:16). Chances are the word covenant never crosses your mind as you admire the resplendent beauty of a rainbow. Perhaps you imagine a pot of gold spilling over at the end, or maybe you contemplate the scientific explanation for such a gorgeous phenomenon, while God calls this magnificent, multicolored bow, a sign. It is a reminder of His everlasting covenant to all generations. The poet William Wordsworth must have understood the rainbow to be a sign, for he took pen in hand and wrote, "My heart leaps when I behold a rainbow in the sky." Perhaps we would feel our hearts leap within us if we were to remember that this majestic bow stretching across the heavens is a sign, an everlasting declaration of love from our heavenly Father.

Being a righteous man set Noah apart from others, yet he was still just a man with feelings and needs familiar to us all. He lived in the desert, and since ships are built at the water's edge, he must have encountered a great deal of ridicule when he began to build an enormous ark miles inland. Human nature being what it is, Noah was probably the butt of many jokes, and the hot topic of party conversations. I can imagine the local teenagers getting their kicks by harassing "the crazy, old man in the desert." However, rejection and ridicule were of no concern to Noah. He cared little what others thought or said about him. With singleness of heart, he purposed to obey God even though he looked foolish in the eyes of the world. And some things never change. Those who choose to walk with God today are often labeled fools by the rest of society. Taking a stand for Christian principles is considered to be not only foolish, but often politically incorrect. Yet, to do less is to seek the approval of men rather than of God. God's Word is crystal clear concerning the fact that those who are in Covenant with Him receive praise from Him, not from men. The apostle Paul realized this and declared, *"If I were still trying to please men, I would not be a bond-servant of Christ"* (Galatians 1:10).

Noah waited one hundred years for the rain to begin, yet Scripture indicates that he never complained, became discouraged, or even doubted. How was that possible? He was just an ordinary man. Yes, but he was an ordinary man who walked with God. The moment Noah surrendered himself to God's will, he became infused with God's supernatural power which enabled him to patiently wait, and turn a deaf ear to the snide remarks. Noah is an excellent example of God keeping those who belong to Him *"in a shelter from the strife of tongues"* (Psalm 31:20).

The environment in which Noah lived was not conducive to walking with God. Today, considerable emphasis is placed upon environment as it relates to an individual's behavior, yet Noah demonstrated that it is possible to walk with God regardless of one's environment. Whether we are raised in a loving family, or forced to fend for ourselves at an early age, the question God asks remains the same: Where is your heart? If our heart is intent on finding God, He will allow us to do so and will enable us to walk with Him as Noah did. It is always a matter of our heart.

Living in an instant society, we expect fast food, immediate gratification, and quick results. Waiting for any reason becomes an intolerable waste of our precious time. It is therefore difficult to imagine Noah patiently waiting one hundred years for the rain to begin. His experience emphasizes the fact that God has a plan and is unfolding it according to His perfect timetable, which usually differs from ours. Although modern society has a way of breeding impatience, God still enables those who are in Covenant with Him to wait for His perfect timing. Taking matters into our own hands and rushing ahead of God can result in our settling for less than God's best, as illustrated by the following story.

Daniel was fresh out of seminary and the assistant pastor of his first church. He and his pregnant wife Linda lived in a small efficiency apartment, and were planning to buy their first home. Since they were accustomed to seeking

God's will in every aspect of their lives, house hunting was no exception. They felt confident that their Covenant Partner knew exactly what they needed and would direct them to the perfect house. They enjoyed the first few months of leisurely house hunting. However, things changed dramatically, when Linda reached her seventh month of pregnancy. With hormones stimulating her nesting instinct and no available outlet, Linda turned into a maternal maniac.

"We have to find a house *now!*" she demanded. "We can't wait any longer." Giving in to the panic, they shifted their searching into high gear, and in a short time found a house that met almost all of their criteria. It certainly wasn't their dream home. It was small, needed to be painted, and had a depressingly outdated kitchen. But it would have to do, since Linda felt as if she were running one step ahead of the stork. They submitted a contract and should have been elated when it was accepted, but they weren't. Instantaneously, they felt the absence of peace and realized that in their haste, they had committed themselves to purchasing a house which fell short of their needs. Their actions were neither rebellious nor sinful, but obviously, they had made a mistake. Amid the stress of the situation, they had simply forgotten about their Covenant Partner and taken matters into their own hands. A wave of nauseating panic hit them. What if they were unable to get out of the contract? What if they had to forfeit their down payment? They were just getting started and could not afford to lose money. Daniel and Linda asked God to forgive their impulsiveness, and to help them. Much to their relief, the owner graciously released them from their commitment, and they prayerfully resumed their search.

The next house they saw was everything they needed and financially within their range. Linda fell in love with it instantly, and Daniel liked the fact that it was within walking distance of his church. It was much more than they had dared to hope for, and they wasted no time in submitting a contract. That night their joy and expectation made sleep almost impossible, but with the rising of the sun, their bubble burst. The realtor called to say that the owner had changed his mind and taken the house off the market. It took a few minutes to process the fact that their dream home was not for sale. They had felt so certain that this was the house for them. How could they have been so mistaken?

With heavy hearts they resumed searching, but found nothing. Day after day Linda prayed and cried as only a hormonal, pregnant woman can. Finally, with tear-stained cheeks she sobbed, "God, I surrender this entire situation to You. Whatever You want is fine with me, even if it means staying in this apartment." And for the first time in weeks, she felt peaceful.

In the days that followed Linda's hormones still wreaked havoc with her determination to patiently wait and trust God. Each time she felt the tension building, she surrendered the situation anew to her Covenant Partner, saturating herself in His peace. Six weeks later, Daniel and Linda received an unexpected phone call from the owner of their dream home. He was now ready to sell and wondered if they might still interested. Wow! They could scarcely contain their excitement, as they made arrangements to meet and complete the paper work. With two weeks to spare, Linda and Daniel found themselves happily settled into their new home, with a beautiful, organized nursery awaiting their new arrival. God's timing is always perfect.

To believers living in Philippi the apostle Paul wrote, *"My God shall supply all your needs according to His riches in glory in Christ Jesus"* (Philippians 4:19). Just as God abundantly supplied Linda and Daniel's need, He continues to do so for all those who are in Covenant with Him. It is just one of His many promises.

Before moving on, permit me to pose one more question. Since Noah was a righteous man and walked with God, why didn't God simply take him to heaven like He did Enoch and Elijah? He could have destroyed the earth and started all over again. Why was it necessary to save Noah and his family? The answer is linked to His Covenant. God promised Eve that the Messiah would come from her seed. If He were going to keep His Covenant promise, He had to preserve her bloodline.

Looking at the genealogy chart, we see that Noah had three sons, Shem, Ham, and Japheth, and that God chose Shem to continue His Covenant chain. Following is a list of the descendants of Shem according to Genesis 11:

When Noah was 502 years old Shem was born

602 years old	Shem's son, Arpachshad was born
637 years old	Arpachshad's son, Shelah was born
672 years old	Shelah's son, Eber was born
706 years old	Eber's son, Peleg was born
736 years old	Peleg's son, Reu was born
768 years old	Reu's son, Serug was born
798 years old	Serug's son, Nahor was born

The Covenant Preserved

827 years old	Nahor's son, Terah was born
897 years old	Terah's son, Abram was born

Noah lived a total of nine hundred and fifty years, witnessing the birth of ten generations of his descendants. This tells us that for over four hundred years, Noah was able to tell his descendants about the flood and God's promise of a coming messiah. I suspect that seeing a rainbow in the sky made their hearts leap, and they stopped whatever they were doing to offer a prayer of thanksgiving.

God instructed Noah and his sons to *"be fruitful and multiply, populate the earth abundantly and multiply in it"* (Genesis 9:7). The Hebrew word translated *populate* in this Scripture means "to creep or to move about." In other words, God was telling them to spread out across the earth. Nevertheless, approximately one hundred years after the flood, the people rebelled. Driven by pride and their own ambition, they opposed God's will by refusing to scatter. Instead, they gathered together in the land of Shinar, saying, *"Come, let us build for ourselves a city, and a tower whose top will reach into heaven, and let us make for ourselves a name; lest we be scattered abroad over the face of the whole earth"* (Genesis 11:4). The tower which they were attempting to build is now called the Tower of Babel, because in response to their defiance, God confused their language and *"scattered them abroad from there over the face of the whole earth; and they stopped building the city"* (Genesis 11:8).

We usually assume this to mean that God halted construction by inhibiting their ability to communicate and then somehow gently relocated them elsewhere, according to their families and languages. A thorough examination reveals this to have been a catastrophic event. The Hebrew word translated *scattered* in this Scripture is *puwts* and it means, "to dash in pieces, to break, to shake into pieces." Further light is shed on this incident by information recorded in Genesis 10:25, which tells us that at this particular time, Shem's great-grandson Eber had a son, and he was named Peleg *"because in his days the earth was divided."* The Hebrew word *peleg* means, "an earthquake, to split, to be divided, to make discordant" and the word translated "divided" also means "to split." These Hebrew definitions give us a more probable explanation of what happened at the Tower of Babel. In addition to confusing their language, Scripture implies that God caused a great earthquake which resulted in the earth dividing into the islands and continents which we know today. Genesis 10:5 says, *"From these the coastlands of the nations were separated into their lands, every one according to his language, according to their families, into their nations."* This is an important fact because it explains why every culture on earth, even the most remote tribe, has a story regarding the flood and a history of blood-covenanting. The details may differ somewhat, but the evidence is there. In H. Clay Trumbull's book, *The Blood Covenant,* he has this to say:

> And so this close and sacred covenant relationship, this rite of blood-friendship, this inter-oneness of life by an inter-oneness of blood, shows itself in the primitive East, and in the wild and pre-historic West; in the frozen North, as in the torrid South. Its traces are everywhere. This fact in itself would seem to point to a

common origin of its various manifestations, in the early oriental home of the now scattered peoples of the world.[1]

Skipping ahead ten generations, we meet the next prominent link in God's Covenant chain, another individual who dared to defy society's norms to walk with God, a man affectionately called the father of the faith—Abraham.

---

[1] *The Blood Covenant* by H. Clay Trumbull. Used by permission of Impact Christian Books, Inc., 332 Leffingwell, Suite 101, Kirkwood, MO 63122. Page 57.

Chapter 6

THE CUTTING OF COVENANT

(Abraham)

Genesis chapter 12 introduces seventy-five-year-old Abram. He and his barren wife Sarai were believers, living in a land of idol worshippers, when God spoke to him, instructing him to leave his home and relatives and to go to a foreign land. God said, *"I will make you a great nation, and I will bless you, and make your name great; and so you shall be a blessing; and I will bless those who bless you, and the one who curses you I will curse, and in you all the families of the earth shall be blessed"* (Genesis 12:2). The phrase "in you all the families of the earth shall be blessed" is particularly important, because it refers to God's Covenant. God was not just promising to give Abram a land, but He was telling him that the Messiah was going to come from his bloodline. Being a righteous man, Abram obeyed, leaving behind all that was familiar and following God to an unknown destination.

Approximately one year later, Abram became troubled over God's prophecy concerning his descendants. He and Sarai still had no children, and Sarai was well past the child-bearing years. Hence Abram asked God if his servant, Eliezer, would be his heir. God's reply was negative.

This man will not be your heir; but one who shall come forth from your own body, he shall be your heir. And He took him outside and said, "Now look toward the heavens, and count the stars, if you are able to count them." And He said to him, "So shall your seed be." (Genesis 15:4–5)

Regarding the land, God said, *"I am the LORD who brought you out of Ur of the Chaldeans to give you this land to possess it"* (Genesis 15:7). While he had God's attention, Abram posed one more question. He asked, *"O Lord God how may I know that I shall possess it?"* (Genesis 15:8). This sounds as if Abram doubted God's word, but that was not the case. He was simply asking how it would happen. "Will you give me this land? Will I have to conquer this land? Will I see this happen in my lifetime, or is the promise for my descendants?" It was a reasonable question, yet God answered Abram in a most unusual way. He instructed Abram to bring Him a three-year-old heifer, a three-year-old female goat, and a three-year-old ram. Then He instructed Abram to cut the animals in two and lay each half opposite the other on the ground. Next, God caused a deep sleep to fall upon Abram and He prophesied concerning the future. He said to him, *"Know for certain that your descendants will be strangers in a land that is not theirs, where they will be enslaved and oppressed four hundred years. But I*

The Cutting of Covenant

will also judge the nation whom they will serve; and afterward they will come out with many possessions. And as for you, you shall go to your fathers in peace; you shall be buried at a good old age" (Genesis 15:13–15). God then proceeded to cut Covenant with Abram. In the form of a smoking, flaming torch, He walked between the pieces of flesh, and Abram joined Him. In cutting this Covenant, God was assuring Abram that he need not concern himself with the details. He was to believe, obey, and watch as God's plan unfolded.

Things went well for about ten years, until Sarai, who was still childless, became impatient and convinced Abram to have a child with her maid, Hagar. God silently watched as they took matters into their own hands in an attempt to fulfill His prophecy. At eighty-six years old, Abram became the father of Ishmael, the son of Hagar, and God remained silent for another thirteen years.

When Abram was ninety-nine years old, twenty-four years after having left his home, God spoke to him again regarding the Covenant. These are God's words recorded in Genesis 17.

1. *I am God Almighty; Walk before Me, and be blameless.*
2. *And I will establish My covenant between Me and you. And I will multiply you exceedingly.*
4. *As for Me, behold, My covenant is with you, And you shall be the father of a multitude of nations.*
7. *And I will establish My covenant between Me and you and your descendants after you throughout their generations for an everlasting covenant, to be God to you and to your descendants after you.*

> 8 And I will give to you and to your descendants after you, the land of your sojournings, all the land of Canaan, for an everlasting possession; and I will be their God.
> 9 Now as for you, you shall keep My covenant, you and your descendants after you throughout their generations.

In restating the Covenant, this time God made it perfectly clear that the child-of-promise would come from the union of Abram and Sarai. Regarding Sarai, He said, *"I will bless her, and indeed I will give you a son by her"* (Genesis 17:16). When Abram suggested that Ishmael be used to fulfill the Covenant, God replied, *"No, Sarah your wife shall bear you a son, and you shall call his name Isaac; and I will establish My Covenant with him for an everlasting Covenant for his descendants after him* (Genesis 17:19).

Why couldn't Ishmael be the one to carry on the Covenant promise? Was he somehow inferior? Of course not. Ishmael could not carry on the Covenant because the conception of this child was going to symbolize the coming Messiah. It had to be miraculous, and Ishmael had been conceived by an ordinary act of the flesh. Inasmuch as Sarai was well past the child-bearing years, Isaac's birth would require God's divine intervention. It was a foreshadowing of the time when a young, unmarried virgin would miraculously be impregnated by God's Holy Spirit and give birth to the fulfillment of His Covenant.

It is important to understand that although Ishmael was not a part of God's Covenant chain, God loved him. He said to Abram, *"As for Ishmael, I have heard you; behold, I will*

The Cutting of Covenant

bless him and will make him fruitful, and will multiply him exceedingly. He shall become the father of twelve princes, and I will make him a great nation" (Genesis 17:20). The Messiah would come from the seed of Isaac; yet when the Covenant was fulfilled, all men, including the descendants of Ishmael, would be included and invited to walk with God.

As further confirmation, God gave Abram a Covenant sign. He said, *"you shall be circumcised in the flesh of your foreskin, and it shall be a sign of the covenant between Me and you. And every male among you who is eight days old shall be circumcised throughout your generation"* (Genesis 17:11–12). You may be thinking that circumcision was a rather odd sign. During biblical times, when a covenant was to be passed on to successive generations, the cut which was made on the body was done as close as possible to the source of paternity. This usually meant that it was done on the upper thigh. God's specific instruction that the cut be made at the source of man's seed graphically depicted the seriousness of His Covenant, and emphasized the fact that it was to be passed from generation to generation.

As a side note, it is interesting that God instructed them to circumcise infants on the eighth day. Since there were no drugs to coagulate the blood, it was essential that they wait until the baby's body was able to produce the necessary prothrombin. We now know that this occurs naturally on the eighth day after birth. Today, circumcision is so widely practiced that it no longer exclusively identifies the descendants of Abraham. Even during biblical times, circumcision lost its Covenant significance. Expressing His displeasure over what had become an empty ritual, God spoke this admonition: *"Circumcise therefore the foreskin of your heart"* (Deuteronomy 10:16 KJV).

In addition to circumcision, God established a memorial of His Covenant. He changed Abram and Sarai's names. At first glance this may seem trivial, but it illustrates the intimacy with which God views His Covenant, for He took a part of Himself and gave it to them. He took the "ah" from His name, Y'HOVAH and added it to their names, changing Abram to Abraham and Sarai to Sarah, attesting once again to the fact that Covenant is all about relationship, not religion. The name changes were an external sign of their internal oneness. We see this same symbolism today in our wedding ceremonies, as the woman takes her husband's name as an outward sign of their internal covenant bond.

The changing of their names reflected God's presence with Abraham and Sarah and placed great responsibility upon them, as the bearing of God's name was not to be taken lightly. In Exodus 20:7 God gave this warning: *"You shall not take the name of the LORD your God in vain, for the LORD will not leave him unpunished who takes His name in vain."* We have a fair idea of what it means to take the LORD'S name in vain. We hear it done every day as people around us use His name profanely, yet it means so much more. The word *vain* in the original Hebrew is *shaw* and it means "nothingness, emptiness, vanity, anything which disappoints the hope which rests upon it." Those who are in Covenant with God today bear His name. They are called *Christians* which means *little Christs* because they are joined to Him by the indwelling of His Holy Spirit. God's message regarding His name remains the same today as it was in biblical times—*"Don't take My name in vain."* A Christian who continues to live in bitterness, hopelessness, greed, immorality, and unforgiveness is taking God's name in vain. That individual is denying the presence and power of God's Holy Spirit within him. Paul said, "*I can do all things through Him who strengthens me*" (Philippians 4:13). By the power of His Holy Spirit, God enables those who belong to Him to live a victorious life, exhibiting the character of Jesus, and keeping Covenant with Him. As the late Oswald Chambers told his students, "It is a positive crime to be weak in God's strength."[1] Why? Because to do so is to take God's name in vain, negating the presence and power of His Holy Spirit. Permit me to share a story which illuminates the importance God places upon His name.

Brenda is a Christian who was deeply hurt by someone she befriended and trusted. This woman lied to her, lied about her, and blatantly seduced Brenda's husband, which caused a great deal of strife to the entire family. Even though she had been a Christian for many years and knew that vengeance belonged to God, Brenda struggled. She was angry—angry with herself, angry with her husband, angry with the other woman, and even angry with God. Friends tried to help, but disregarding their advice and God's Word, Brenda concocted a revengeful plan of her own.

The other woman drove a small, white sports car. Brenda's plan was to paint red A's all over the car so that this woman would face public humiliation. As she was driving to the paint store, God spoke to her from these verses in

---

[1] *My Utmost for His Highest* by Oswald Chambers © 1935 by Dodd Mead & Co., renewed © 1963 by the Oswald Chambers Publications Assn., Ltd., and is used by permission of Discovery House Publishers, Box 3566, Grand Rapids, MI 49501. All rights reserved. Page 105.

Genesis, *"Why are you angry? And why has your countenance fallen? If you do well, will not your countenance be lifted up? And if you do not do well, sin is crouching at the door and its desire is for you, but you must master it"* (Genesis 4:6–7). The venom of bitterness spewed forth as Brenda dared to sass God. "God, You know very well why I'm angry. I have every reason to be angry. In fact, I am angry with You for allowing this to happen," she barked, as she squealed her car into a parking space.

Later that evening, as she made plans to carry out her scheme, God spoke to Brenda again. This time, He asked no questions, but instead gave a very clear warning, "Don't take My name in vain," He said. "I will not hold you guiltless if you take My name in vain. Everyone knows you are a Christian. You have the power to make it through this. Do not take My name in vain." Brenda stood frozen in her tracks. She could not knowingly, willfully, and defiantly deny the power of God's presence within her and deliberately disgrace His name. This was rock bottom. All the bitterness and anger that was festering within her heart erupted in anguished sobs and tears of repentance. And God was there. Meeting her at the point of her weakness, He began to strengthen Brenda, heal her, and teach her how to extend forgiveness in this difficult situation. It is a beautiful picture of God's Covenant in action! When Brenda tried to ignore her Covenant Partner by going off on a revengeful tangent, God lovingly reached out to remind her that she belonged to Him. The instant she chose to honor her Covenant Partner by refusing to take His name in vain, God was there to give her everything she needed. He will do the same for you and me.

The Cutting of Covenant

The apostle Paul exhibited this understanding of Covenant when he said, *"for in Him we live and move and have our being"* (Acts 17:28 KJV). There is absolutely no separation between spiritual life and secular life for those who are in Covenant with God. The relationship is reflected in every aspect. In a St. Louis Post Dispatch newspaper article written about Michael Gerson, speechwriter for President George W. Bush, Michael was remembered and praised by one of his high school teachers who said, "Michael recognized that how you act should reflect what you believe, and there should be a connection." This is the Covenant relationship—living, moving, and having our being in Christ. All the while we are abiding in Him, He is giving us love, direction, wisdom, healing, guidance, strength, comfort, protection, peace, joy, forgiveness, and the promise of eternal life with Him. Who could ask for anything more?

Abraham's life is much like Noah's in that it illustrates the importance of waiting upon God. It took twenty-five years for God's promise of a son to be realized, and things became complicated when they took matters into their own hands. Just like us, Abraham and Sarah found waiting to be difficult. Waiting when God remains silent is always a test. Spiritual maturity is best measured not by one's ability to do great things, but by one's ability to wait patiently when God chooses to remain silent. Christians who have walked many a mile with their Covenant Partner are not easily given to complaining or rushing ahead of God. They have learned to wait and trust, knowing *"that God causes all things to work together for good to those who love God, to those who are called according to His purpose"* (Romans 8:28). They are able to *"rest in the LORD and wait patiently for Him"* (Psalm

37:7). These individuals are not saints. They are just ordinary men and women who have come to understand that Christianity is a Covenant relationship.

God said to Abraham, "*Walk before Me and be blameless and I will establish My covenant between Me and you*" (Genesis 17:1). God did not ask that Abraham fast longer, pray harder, or offer more sacrifices. He simply told him to *walk* before Him and be blameless. The Hebrew word for *walk* used in this Scripture is figuratively applied to an individual's relationship with God, and therefore, shows us once again that God's focus is always on the relationship. His plan is that we become joined to Him, and simply walk with Him through life. Abraham's obedience, his questions, and even his mistakes were all a part of sharing his life with God; nothing has changed. It is the same for us today. All of us have the opportunity and the privilege of entering into God's Covenant and sharing our lives with Him. The invitation has been extended—the choice to accept it or reject it is ours.

Chapter 7

TRUSTING IN GOD'S COVENANT

(Abraham's Test)

When Isaac was probably in his teenage years, Abraham faced a test which demonstrated not only his faithfulness to God, but also his unshakable grasp of God's Covenant. Genesis 22:2 records God giving the following instructions to Abraham: *"Take now your son, your only son, whom you love, Isaac, and go to the land of Moriah; and offer him there as a burnt offering on one of the mountains of which I will tell you."* What a bizarre thing to ask of Abraham! God loathed human sacrifice. How do you suppose you might have responded had you been in Abraham's shoes? Genesis 22:3 explains what Abraham did. He *"rose early in the morning and saddled his donkey, and took two of his young men with him and Isaac his son; and he split wood for the burnt offering, and arose and went to the place of which God had told him."*

It is interesting to note what Abraham did *not* do. He did not procrastinate. He did not cry, or beg God to reconsider, even though the death of a child is every parent's worst nightmare. He did not tell Sarah about it, nor did he discuss it with his men. What enabled Abraham to behave as he did? Hebrews 11:19 tells us that *"He [Abraham] considered that God is able to raise men even from the dead."* Allow me to suggest that Abraham knew more than the fact that God could raise Isaac from the dead. Because he understood what it meant to be in Covenant with God, there was never a doubt in his mind that God *would* raise Isaac from the dead. Abraham's faith was based on one sure thing—the fact that God always keeps His Covenant. Long before Isaac's birth, God made it perfectly clear that Isaac was to be the next link in His Covenant chain. We read this in Genesis 17:19–21: *"Sarah, your wife, shall bear you a son, and you shall call his name Isaac; and I will establish My Covenant with him for an everlasting Covenant for his descendants after him. And as for Ishmael, I have heard you; behold I will bless him and will make him fruitful, and multiply him exceedingly. He shall become the father of twelve princes and I will make him a great nation. But My Covenant I will establish with Isaac, whom Sarah will bear to you at this season next year."*

Remembering and believing these words enabled Abraham to bind Isaac and place him on the altar. He did not understand why God was asking him to do this thing, nor did he know how the details would be worked out, but he knew that Isaac would live, because he knew God to be a Covenant-keeping God.

Did you notice that Abraham was not free to choose the location for this sacrifice? God instructed him to go to the land of Moriah and there he would be shown the exact spot. Scripture tells us that Abraham traveled for three days, and *"on the third day Abraham raised his eyes and saw the place from a distance"* (Genesis 22:4). Why was God so particular about the place? Did it somehow involve His Covenant? Yes, I believe it did. Had this been merely a test of Abraham's obedience, the sacrifice could have been done anywhere. This location was chosen by God because of its Covenant implications.

Fourteen generations after Abraham, God commanded King David to build an altar on Mount Moriah, on a parcel of land owned by a Jebusite named Ornan. David purchased the land, and built the altar, which then became the tabernacle of God for all the tribes of Israel. After David's death, his son Solomon erected the temple on this same site, making Mount Moriah the place where God historically dwelt among His people. There is more! Calvary, the crucifixion site of Jesus Christ, was also located on Mount Moriah. Are you beginning to see the pieces coming together? Some might call this merely coincidence, but with God there is no such thing. He is the master of detail. By taking Abraham to Mount Moriah, where fourteen generations later His temple would be erected, and forty-two generations later His own Son would be crucified, God beautifully illustrated the continuity of His Covenant. His promise to Abraham; the Law, which He would cut with the Israelites; and the New Covenant, which would be cut in the blood of His only son, Jesus Christ is one, continuous, unbroken chain!

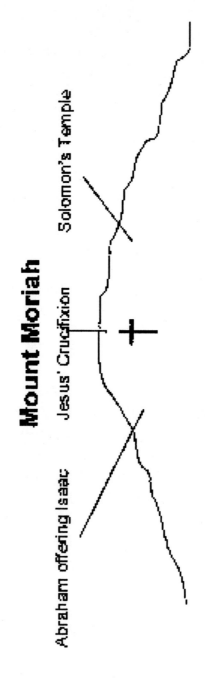

Trusting in God's Covenant

As Abraham stood with his knife poised only inches above Isaac's heart *"the angel of the LORD called to him from heaven, saying 'Abraham, Abraham!'"* Abraham answered, *"Here I am."* To his great relief, the angel said, *"Do not stretch out your hand against the lad, and do nothing to him; for now I know that you fear God, since you have not withheld your son, your only son, from Me"* (Genesis 22:11–12). A ram, caught in a nearby thicket, caught Abraham's attention. After killing it, he offered it in place of his son, and named the site Jehovah-Jireh. Afterwards, God said to Abraham, *"because you have done this thing and have not withheld your son, your only son, indeed I will greatly bless you, and I will greatly multiply your seed as the stars of the heavens, and as the sand which is on the seashore; and your seed shall possess the gate of their enemies. And in your seed all the nations of the earth shall be blessed, because you have obeyed My voice"* (Genesis 22:16–18). Notice that God was restating His Covenant promise. All the nations of the earth would be blessed through Abraham, because the coming Messiah would be one of his descendants. Without a doubt, this was the greatest blessing God could bestow upon Abraham; yet, He did even more. As Abraham stood on Mount Moriah, only seconds removed from the most horrendous test of his life, God blessed him with a prophetic vision. This vision allowed him to perceive how the Covenant would be fulfilled. He saw how God was going to sacrifice His only son, Jesus Christ, on Mount Moriah, just as he had been asked to do. I believe this to be true for two reasons. First, because Jesus told the Jews, *"Your father, Abraham, rejoiced to see My day; and he saw it, and was glad"* (John 8:56). Abraham lived hundreds of years before the time of Jesus, so the only way he could have seen Jesus was through a divine, prophetic vision. Secondly, I believe Abraham saw this vision because he renamed the site "Jehovah-Jireh" which means "the Lord will provide," indicting that there on Mount Moriah the Lord would provide the sacrificial Lamb of God to offer restoration of the lost relationship to all mankind.

Only hours before going to the cross, Jesus shared bread and wine with His disciples, saying *"This is My blood of the Covenant, which is to be shed on behalf of many"* (Mark 14:24). There would be no animals involved in the cutting of this Covenant. Jesus would cut this Covenant in His own blood, making it possible for men to once again walk with God. Nevertheless, having this information is not enough.

If you were to read a biography about President George W. Bush, you would learn a great deal about him and his family. However, if you then presented yourself at the White House, claiming to be a personal friend of the president, you would be denied admittance. Like Jesus, President Bush would be forced to say, "I never knew you," because having information about someone does not constitute a relationship. God has made it clear that Christianity is an intimate, covenant relationship of the heart, requiring the participation of both parties. Laying aside His divinity, Jesus willingly put on our robe of flesh. After declaring, *"Greater love has no one than this, that one lay down his life for his friends"* (John 15:13) he suffered and died to cut the Covenant in His own blood. After His resurrection, He sent the Holy Spirit to indwell all those who choose to be His Covenant partners. God has done, and continues to do His part. Consequently, He asks nothing more, and can accept nothing less than our laying down control of our lives to become one with Him. This is the bedrock of Christianity. It is a relationship, not a religion.

Abraham had unquestioning trust in the fact that God always keeps His Covenant. You and I may have that same assurance since God said, *"I, the LORD, do not change"* (Malachi 3:6) and *"Jesus Christ is the same yesterday and today, yes and forever"* (Hebrews 13:8). Like Abraham, we may not understand why God allows some things to occur, but if He is our Covenant Partner, we have the assurance that He loves us and is continually working things out for our good. Whenever God's Covenant partners are tempted to worry or be fearful, trusting in His promises offers the same assurance and peace that Abraham had.

Here are just a few of the many promises God has given to His Covenant partners:

- *If any of you lacks wisdom, let him ask of God, who gives to all men generously and without reproach and it will be given to him* (James 1:5).

This is one of my favorite verses because it is so simple and practical. If you need wisdom, just ask for it. God never fails to give wisdom to His Covenant partners when they ask, as illustrated by the following story.

Sandra operates a home-based secretarial service; therefore, computer savvy and upgraded equipment are essential to her business. However, her last upgrade gave her an opportunity to test the validity of James 1:5. After working for hours on a client's project, she inadvertently removed the entire file from her screen. Panic gave way to nausea as she tried in vain to retrieve her work. Finally, remembering God's promise in James 1:5, she prayed. In answer to her distress call, that internal, still, small voice instructed her to turn off the computer. "No way," she argued. "If I turn it off, I will lose everything." Yet when the internal directive persisted, she finally capitulated and began shutting down the computer. During the process, a "Find" button appeared on the screen. She clicked on it, typed in the name of her file, and retrieved the misplaced document. Her relief erupted in shouts of praise to God. Now admittedly in the scope of life, a computer problem is relatively insignificant. On the other hand, it is often those little, everyday malfunctions that frustrate us, causing us to appreciate God's promise in James 1:5. God gives wisdom whenever His Covenant partners request it, because it is a part of being in Covenant with Him.

- *God causes all things to work together for good to those who love God, to those who are called according to His purpose* (Romans 8:28).

As we continue looking at the lives of those who carried God's Covenant message to their generations, the truth of this statement will be exemplified over and over again.

- *If you abide in Me, and My words abide in you, ask whatever you wish, and it shall be done for you* (John 15:7).

What a wonderful promise! But what happens when we ask for something that is contrary to God's will? This is where we experience His kindness, and come to appreciate the intricacy of His divine presence within us. When we ask for something which is not in accordance with God's will for us, and if we surrender this desire to Him, He changes our hearts so that we no longer desire it. This spares us the anguish of longing for something which is not in our best interest. It is just another miraculous aspect of walking in Covenant with Him. If you are a Christian and feeling frustrated because of having asked for something which you have not received, now would be a good time to surrender that desire to the Lord. God never violates our free will. Therefore, our hearts cannot be changed until we relinquish control.

- *The thief comes only to steal and kill and destroy, I came that they might have life, and might have it abundantly* (John 10:10).

The abundance Jesus spoke of was not an abundance of material possessions, but rather an abundance of Himself—walking with Him, and having our lives enriched every day by His presence within us. This abundant life begins the moment we enter into Covenant with Him and continues beyond physical death into eternity. God loves everyone, but only His Covenant partners have the heart capacity to recognize and receive it. Like raindrops splashing off a windowpane, His blessings are repelled by a hardened heart.

- *If we confess our sins, He is faithful and just to forgive us our sins and to cleanse us from all unrighteousness* (1 John 1:9).

We will be looking closely at this promise in chapter 12.

- *He will cover you with His pinions, and under His wings you may seek refuge. His faithfulness is a shield and bulwark* (Psalm 91:4).

Remember, a covenant provides protection for the parties involved. Therefore, since Christianity is a covenant, God's sheltering wings are a wall of protection around those who belong to Him, as seen in the following story.

Lisa lovingly tucked the quilt around her sleeping fifteen-month old daughter, snapped the side of the crib into the upright position, and tiptoed from the room. Ten minutes later, she heard the baby cry. *"She's fed, changed, and safe in her bed,"* Lisa surmised. *"I'm going to let her cry herself back to sleep."*

Momentarily, the crying stopped, and Lisa resumed doing her chores. Then, all of a sudden, she knew that something was wrong. "Check on the baby, NOW!" an internal voice commanded, sending Lisa running towards the nursery. Upon reaching the stairs, she saw her child teetering on the brink of a long staircase. Lisa raced up the stairs, scooped the child into her arms, and thanked God for His sheltering wings.

- *I am with you always, even to the end of the age* (Matthew 28:20).

Trusting in God's Covenant

- *I will never desert you, nor will I ever forsake you* (Hebrews 13:5).

God's Covenant is unconditional. He is the eternal companion of all who join themselves to Him. He picks them up when they fall, He comforts them when they are hurting, He strengthens them when they are weak, He encourages them when they are downcast, and He disciplines them when they get off track. Little by little, day after day, He teaches them how to walk with Him and experience the joy of being His Covenant partner.

Abraham is often called the Father of the Faith. Because he understood the Covenant relationship; he trusted God, no matter what. When you and I grasp the meaning of being God's Covenant partner, our faith can become as unshakable as Abraham's, because God has not changed. The abundant life, promised by Jesus, remains available to all who choose to walk in Covenant with Him.

Chapter 8

ABIDING IN GOD'S COVENANT

(Isaac)

In considering the test God gave to Abraham, our attention is quite naturally drawn to Abraham. We scrutinize his behavior, searching for a key to unlock the secret of his unshakable trust in God. But what about Isaac? We know that as Isaac carried the wood on his back and journeyed with Abraham, he was aware that things were deviating from the norm. *"Where is the lamb for the burnt offering?"* he asked. *"God will provide for Himself the lamb for the burnt offering, my son,"* Abraham reassured him (Genesis 22:7–8).

As Isaac lay bound with Abraham's knife poised only inches above his heart, what was going through his mind? Was he terrified? Scripture indicates that he did not try to escape, or plead for his life. He did not scream, "Father this cannot be of God. God abhors human sacrifice." Isaac remained silent! How could he do that? Was he in shock, or did his silence indicate something more profound? Did Isaac's understanding of God's Covenant enable him to look beyond the horror of the moment to a God who could be trusted to keep His Covenant? Although we have no way of knowing what was going through Isaac's mind, this incident does shed considerable light on his heart. Isaac's miraculous birth made him an extraordinary individual, but he was also unique in that he loved God and had apparently learned unquestioning obedience by observing his father. He knew and believed that God had a plan which would find its fulfillment in his descendants. All the nations of the earth were going to be blessed by the Messiah, who was coming from the seed of Isaac to offer restoration of the lost relationship to all mankind. Based on that truth, he was confident that no matter what happened that day on Mount Moriah, he would live, marry, and have descendants.

When the time came for Isaac to marry, Abraham sent one of his servants to relatives living in Mesopotamia, instructing him to choose a wife for Isaac. As the servant prepared to depart, Abraham encouraged him with these words, *"The Lord, the God of heaven who took me from my father's house and from the land of my birth, and who spoke to me, and who swore to me saying, 'To your descendants I will give this land', He will send His angel before you, and you will take a wife for my son from there"* (Genesis 24:7). Upon arriving in Mesopotamia, Abraham's servant paused to ask for God's help.

> *O LORD, the God of my master, Abraham, please grant me success today, and show loving kindness to my master*

> *Abraham. Behold, I am standing by the spring, and the daughters of the men of the city are coming out to draw water; now may it be that the girl to whom I say, 'Please let down your jar so that I may drink,' and who answers, 'Drink, and I will water your camels also;' may she be the one whom Thou hast appointed for Thy servant Isaac; and by this I shall know that Thou hast shown loving kindness to my master"* (Genesis 24:12–14).

Even before he finished praying, he was approached by Abraham's great niece, Rebekah, who responded to his request for a drink by saying, *"Drink, my lord and I will draw also for your camels,"* perfectly echoing his request. (Genesis 24:18–19)

The union of Rebekah and Isaac was truly a match made in heaven. They loved each other dearly and had only one problem—Rebekah was barren. She was God's choice, and His Covenant was to be passed to Isaac's descendants, so what were they to do? With a heavy heart Isaac brought this pressing need to God's attention, but God did not share Isaac's sense of urgency. From His perspective, things were progressing according to plan. Consequently, years passed and the sadness in Rebekah's eyes mirrored the longing within Isaac's own heart, as he prayed unceasingly for a son. Finally, after twenty years of waiting, God healed Rebekah's barrenness, blessing her with twins. During the pregnancy, God said to her, *"Two nations are in your womb; and two peoples shall be separated from your body and one people shall be stronger than the other; and the older shall serve the younger"* (Genesis 25:23). Rebekah could not grasp the implications of God's prediction, but she kept the prophecy hidden in her heart to recall it years later, as she watched God's plan unfolding.

Isaac now had a wife and descendants, but God had not yet spoken to him regarding the Covenant. A severe famine, which threatened his life and that of his family, became the catalyst God used to confirm Isaac's position as the next link in the Covenant chain. He was preparing to move his family to safety in Egypt, when the Lord appeared to him, instructed him to remain in Canaan, and spoke to him regarding the Covenant. "*Do not go down to Egypt,*" God said. "*Stay in the land of which I shall tell you. Sojourn in this land and I will be with you and bless you, for to you and to your seed I will give all these lands, and I will establish the oath which I swore to your father, Abraham. And I will multiply your seed as the stars of heaven and will give your seed all these lands; and by your seed all the nations of the earth shall be blessed; because Abraham obeyed Me and kept My charge, My commandments, My statutes, and My laws*" (Genesis 26:2–5). Isaac remained in the land of the Philistines, where God not only saved his life, but blessed him with such wealth that the Philistines regarded him as a threat. That being the case, the Philistine king eventually ordered him to leave. Isaac must have felt heavy-hearted and somewhat perplexed about leaving the land which God had clearly promised to him and his descendants, because as he prepared to depart, God encouraged him with these words: "*I am the God of your father, Abraham; do not fear, for I am with you. I will bless you, and multiply your descendants, for the sake of My servant Abraham*" (Genesis 26:24).

Scripture gives no information regarding Isaac's interaction with his sons during their childhood. We are simply told that the firstborn was named Esau and the second was called Jacob (Genesis 25:25–26). *"When the boys grew up, Esau became a skillful hunter, a man of the field; but Jacob was a peaceful man, living in tents"* (Genesis 25:27). *"Isaac loved Esau, because he had a taste for game; but Rebekah loved Jacob"* (Genesis 25:28). Perhaps Rebekah was influenced by God's prophetic words given prior to their births. Nevertheless, since Esau was the firstborn, the birthright legally belonged to him.

A birthright was the inheritance given to the eldest son. It usually involved family leadership (2 Chronicles 21:3), a double portion of the father's wealth (Deuteronomy 21:17), and a special consecration to God (Exodus 22:29). This consecration was especially meaningful, because it was the continuance of God's promise that the Messiah would come from the lineage of Abraham. Perhaps the reason God told Rebekah that the older son would serve the younger was that prior to their births, God knew their hearts. He knew that Esau had a rebellious spirit and would never honor Him. Therefore, He instituted another plan, which began to unfold one seemingly ordinary day when Esau returned from hunting. Feeling famished and seeing Jacob cooking a pot of stew, Esau demanded that it be given to him. *"First sell me your birthright,"* Jacob promptly responded. The birthright may have long been a bone of contention between them, or possibly it was God's providence that caused Jacob to make such an extreme suggestion. Nevertheless, Esau felt that he had nothing to lose. He had no regard for God's Covenant, and was confident that he could easily overpower his mild-mannered brother and take whatever he wanted.

Therefore, concerned only with satisfying his immediate hunger, Esau agreed.

It appears, however, that Isaac knew nothing about the exchange. When he became quite elderly, with his vision nearly gone, he wanted to pronounce the birthright blessing before his death. Calling Esau to his side, he said, *"Please take your gear, your quiver, and your bow, and go out to the field and hunt game for me; and prepare a savory dish for me such as I love, and bring it to me that I may eat, so that my soul may bless you before I die"* (Genesis 27:3–4). This was Esau's chance to exhibit some integrity and inform his father of the exchange. Instead, he said nothing, and hurried to procure the requested game. Rebekah overheard the conversation and while Esau was hunting, she helped Jacob to disguise himself as Esau and receive the blessing. Technically, Jacob had every right to the blessing, but when Esau returned, he became furious and vowed to kill his brother. In an effort to save Jacob's life, Isaac sent him to Mesopotamia with instructions to take a wife from among his relatives still living there. Esau, on the other hand, brought much *"grief to Isaac and Rebekah"* by marrying two Hittite women and one of Ishmael's daughters (Genesis 26:34–35).

In looking at Isaac's life, it is easy to see that although he was the long-awaited child of promise, he experienced needs and disappointments like any other man, yet he never complained. Isaac personified the words "wait on the Lord." He knew that God was with him, would provide for him, and protect him. Consequently, amid every situation, he turned to his Covenant Partner, and God proved Himself to be ever faithful.

At this point, you may be thinking, *so what!* That was a long time ago and Isaac was a special individual. We cannot expect God to meet our needs today, can we? Yes, we can! Absolutely! If we are in Covenant with God through Jesus Christ, He has promised to meet our every need. Paul wrote to New Covenant believers in Philippi saying, *"My God shall supply all your needs according to His riches in glory in Christ Jesus"* (Philippians 4:19). Notice that Paul used the word *needs* not *wants*. We have a tendency to confuse the two, but God has no such problem. If God were a genie, who dutifully granted our every wish, we would find ourselves in horrendous circumstances. Thankfully, He is the epitome of love, protecting us at times even from ourselves. Notice also that the Scripture says that God meets ALL the needs of those who belong to Him, not just those that are life-threatening, or too big for us to handle. Over and over again in His Word, God confirms His willingness and desire to meet the needs of His Covenant partners. The following Scriptures are only a few of the many promises God has given to those who choose to walk in Covenant with Him.

When God's Covenant partner needs Provision, God says

> *O fear the LORD, you His saints; For to those who fear Him, there is no want. The young lions do lack and suffer hunger; but they who seek the LORD shall not be in want of any good thing* (Psalm 34:9–10).

> *Do not be anxious then, saying, 'What shall we eat?' or 'What shall we drink?' or with what shall we clothe ourselves.'*

For all these things the Gentiles eagerly seek; for your Heavenly Father knows that you need all these things. But seek first His kingdom and righteousness; and all these things shall be added to you (Matthew 6:31–33).

I have been young and now I am old; yet I have not seen the righteous forsaken or his descendants begging bread (Psalm 37:25).

The LORD will accomplish what concerns me (Psalm 138:8).

When God's Covenant partner needs Emotional Healing, God says

The righteous cry and the LORD hears, and delivers them out of all their troubles. The LORD is near the brokenhearted, and saves those who are crushed in spirit. Many are the afflictions of the righteous, but the LORD delivers him out of them all (Psalm 34:17–19).

He heals the brokenhearted and binds up their wounds (Psalm 147:3).

When God's Covenant partner needs Protection, God says

He who dwells in the shelter of the Most High, will abide in the shadow of the Almighty (Psalm 91:1).

He will not allow your foot to slip. He who keeps you will not slumber. The LORD will guard your going out and your coming in from this time forth and forever (Psalm 121:3,8).

He will cover you with His pinions, and under His wings you may seek refuge; His faithfulness is a shield and bulwark (Psalm 91:4).

He will give His angels charge concerning you, to guard you in all your ways (Psalm 91:11).

The name of the LORD is a strong tower, the righteous runs into it and is safe (Proverbs 18:10).

Thou art my hiding place; Thou dost preserve me from trouble. Thou doest surround me with songs of deliverance (Psalm 32:7).

When God's Covenant partner needs Courage, God says

Be strong and courageous, do not be afraid or tremble at them, for the LORD your God is the one who goes with you. He will not fail you nor forsake you (Deuteronomy 31:6).

God has not given us a spirit of fear, but of power and love and a sound mind (2 Timothy 1:7 KJV).

Do not be afraid of sudden fear, nor of the onslaught of the wicked when it comes, for the Lord will be your confidence, and will keep your foot from being caught (Proverbs 3:25–26).

When God's Covenant partner needs Wisdom, God says

If any of you lacks wisdom, let him ask of God, who gives to all men generously and without reproach, and it will be given to him (James 1:5).

The Lord gives wisdom; from His mouth come knowledge and understanding. He stores up sound wisdom for the upright. He is a shield to those who walk in integrity (Proverbs 2:6–7).

When God's Covenant partner needs Guidance, God says

I will instruct you and teach you in the way which you should go. I will counsel you with My eye upon you (Psalm 32:8, 10).

"This is the covenant which I will make with the house of Israel after those days," declares the Lord. "I will put My law within them; and on their heart I will write it; and I will be their God, and they shall be My people. And they shall not teach again, each man his neighbor and each man his brother, saying, 'Know the Lord,' for they shall all know Me, from the least of them to the greatest of them," declares the Lord, "for I will forgive their iniquity, and their sin I will remember no more" (Jeremiah 31:33–34).

When God's Covenant partner needs Physical Healing, God says

> *My son, give attention to my words; incline your ear to my sayings, do not let them depart from your sight, keep them in the midst of your heart for they are life to those who find them and health to all their whole body* (Proverbs 4:20–22).

> *Is anyone among you sick? Let him call for the elders of the church, and let them pray over him, anointing him with oil in the name of the Lord; and the prayer offered in faith will restore the one who is sick, and the Lord will raise him up, and if he has committed sins, they will be forgiven* (James 5:14–15).

It is wise to remember that Rebekah's healing took time. In every situation there is the element of God's perfect timing. Noah waited one hundred years for the flood to come, Abraham and Sarah waited twenty-five years for Isaac to be born, and Isaac and Rebekah had to wait twenty years for her barrenness to be healed. Those twenty years must have been a heartbreaking time for them, month after month marked by expectation and disappointment. Abraham probably found it to be a painful déjà vu. I can imagine him kneeling beside Isaac with his arm around his son's shoulder encouraging him, "Pray my son. God will answer you. Wait, my son. Don't make the same mistake I made." If Abraham could speak to us today, I believe he would encourage us with the same words: pray and wait.

The Forgotten Covenant

Throughout the Scriptures, God speaks to those of every generation, reminding them that He is the provider, protector, healer, strength, and eternal companion of all who choose to be His Covenant partner. In Psalm 138:8 the psalmist wrote, "*The Lord will accomplish what concerns me.*" Those secret dreams that lay gently on your heart, and the unspoken fears that weigh heavily upon your mind are of concern to God. He is concerned about everything that is of concern to you. It could be a loved one, an illness, a relationship, a job, or any one of the heartaches that touch our lives, but God's Covenant partners have the assurance that He is overseeing everything that concerns them.

You may be single and concerned about finding the right mate. If so, pray and wait. God will lead you to the love of your life. He did it for Isaac, and He will do the same for you. Psalm 37:4 says to "*delight yourself in the Lord; and He will give you the desires of your heart.*" That Hebrew word *delight* means to be soft or pliable. In other words, don't be rigid. Relinquish control, abandoning yourself completely to God, and allow Him to direct your future.

Perhaps you find yourself empathizing with Rebekah. Month after month you have prayed and hoped, only to face disappointment. You wonder if God even hears the cry of your heart. Of course He does! Jesus said, "Ask, *and it shall be given to you; seek, and you shall find; knock, and it shall be opened to you. For every one who asks receives, and he who seeks finds, and to him who knocks it shall be opened*" (Matthew 7:7–8). The tense of the Greek verbs *ask*, *seek* and *knock* indicates that believers are to ask, and to keep on asking; to seek, and to keep on seeking; to knock, and to keep on knocking. Just like Noah, Abraham, and Isaac, we are not to give up, because God hears and answers in His perfect timing. First John 5:13–14 reiterates this truth again, *"if we ask anything according to His will, He hears us, and if we know that He hears us in whatever we ask, we know that we have the requests which we have asked from Him."*

Perhaps you can identify with Isaac's fear of the famine. For any number of reasons you may be concerned about the future. On September 11, 2001 airliners filled with passengers were hijacked by terrorists and flown into the World Trade Center Towers in New York City, and the Pentagon in Washington, DC. A third plane, believed to have been headed for the White House, crashed in a Pennsylvania field. This unthinkable act of insanity instantly changed our lives, forcing us to view the future with an uncertainty and a keen awareness of how little control we have. Yet amid the uncertainty, those who are in Covenant with God find peace in the assurance that God is in control and *"No good thing does He withhold from those who walk uprightly"* (Psalm 84:11). In times of laughter and tears, we know that God *"is able to do exceeding, abundantly beyond all that we ask or think, according to the power that works within us,"* when we belong to Him (Ephesians 3:20).

Some years ago, as part of a missionary team, I was scheduled to fly from St. Louis to Los Angeles and there board a chartered flight to Manila. When our departure from St. Louis became delayed, I grew anxious, knowing that I would have only minutes to make the Los Angeles connection. While en route, I learned that there was no ground transportation to the charter terminal, which meant that I would have to exit the main building and run to make the connection.

"God, please help me make this flight," I prayed as I raced to the baggage claim area. Nervously waiting amid a sea of humanity, I watched as the bags slowly slipped on to the carousel. Finally, spotting mine, I apologetically pushed my way through the crowd, "Excuse me, pardon me, I am so sorry." However, before reaching my bag, something extraordinary happened. Seemingly out of nowhere came a huge, black arm that reached across my shoulder and picked up my bag. Stunned, I watched as this enormous black stranger holding my luggage slowly turned to face the crowd. As he did so, the throng parted before him like the Red Sea, and I followed along at his heels, as if obeying his unspoken command. Upon reaching the exit, he abruptly stopped, turned, and placed the bag into my hands. Without a second thought, I thanked him and took off running. Only after safely aboard the chartered flight did I relax and begin to address the barrage of questions in my mind. Who was that black man? Why did he help me? How did he know which bag was mine? How did he know where I needed to go, and why hadn't I been upset by a complete stranger taking my luggage? Searching for the answers, I mentally retraced my steps, but the entire episode seemed surreal. It was like trying to recall a dream where even the most bizarre seems perfectly normal. Although I was never able to recall the man's face, he had two distinct, unforgettable characteristics. First, his size. He was the largest man I had ever seen. Standing beside him, I felt as if I were eye level with his waist. Secondly, and more importantly, I will forever remember the peace that emanated from him. Amid this potentially stressful situation, without uttering a word, this tall, dark stranger had assured me that everything was as it should be.

This incident occurred many years ago, yet I think of it occasionally and smile at the thought of God sending that mysterious, huge angel to assist in my time of need. I share this experience with you because it illustrates the fact that God, as our Covenant Partner, is concerned about all of our needs, even the small ones. And He uses the riches of heaven (including His largest angels!) to meet the needs of those who belong to Him. Why does He do that? He does it because we are in a Covenant relationship.

That being the case, it should be understood that the reverse is likewise true. Those who are in Covenant with God give their all—their time, their strength, and their resources—to meet His needs. What could God possibly need? Often He needs two arms to hold and comfort an individual who is hurting. In crises situations, He needs those who are willing to go beyond their own comfort zones to provide physical, emotional, and spiritual relief to the victims. He needs individuals who will be there to strengthen the weak and befriend the lonely. And every day He needs His Covenant partners to be lights, beacons of hope and encouragement to those who are searching for Him with all their hearts.

Chapter 9

LIVING IN THE COVENANT

(Jacob)

With Esau's threat ringing in his ears, Jacob hurriedly left for Mesopotamia, pausing only long enough to receive Isaac's blessing: *"May God Almighty bless you and make you fruitful and multiply you, that you may become a company of peoples. May He also give you the blessing of Abraham, to you and to your descendants with you; that you may possess the land of your sojournings, which God gave to Abraham"* (Genesis 28:3–4).

During the journey, God appeared to Jacob in a dream and spoke to him regarding the Covenant. He said, *"I am the LORD, the God of your father Abraham and the God of Isaac; the land on which you lie, I will give it to you and to your descendants. Your descendants shall also be like the dust of the earth, and you shall spread out to the west and to the east and to the north and to the south; and in you and in your seed shall all the families of the earth be blessed. And behold,*

The Forgotten Covenant

I am with you and will keep you wherever you go, and will bring you back to this land; for I will not leave you until I have done what I have promised you" (Genesis 28:13–15).

Jacob was deeply touched by God's visitation, and responded by setting up a stone pillar as a memorial, and making the following promise: *"If God will be with me and will keep me on this journey that I take, and will give me food to eat and garments to wear and I return to my father's house in safety, then the LORD will be my God. And this stone, which I have set up as a pillar, will be God's house, and of all that Thou dost give me I will surely give a tenth to Thee"* (Gen. 28:20–22). Jacob renamed the site on which this occurred Bethel, which means the House of God.

Upon arriving in Haran, Jacob was met by his uncle Laban and his two daughters, Leah and Rachel. Rachel was the most beautiful woman Jacob had ever seen, and he could not take his eyes off of her. It was love at first sight! When Laban offered him a job, Jacob enthusiastically accepted, realizing that it would afford him an excuse to be near the love of his life. He was so smitten with Rachel that he worked a month without realizing that he had not been paid. Calling this to his attention, Laban said, *"Because you are my relative, should you therefore serve me for nothing? Tell me, what shall your wages be?"* (Genesis 29:15). Seizing the moment, Jacob quickly replied, *"I will serve you seven years for your younger daughter Rachel"* (Genesis 29:18). Laban agreed, and Jacob couldn't have been happier.

The seven years slipped away like an enchanted dream, but dark clouds loomed upon the horizon. On the day of their wedding, Laban reneged on his promise. Instead of permitting Jacob to marry Rachel, he substituted Leah, explaining that it was improper for the younger daughter to marry before the eldest. Then he cleverly offered a solution. If Jacob would complete the bridal week with Leah, and commit himself to an additional seven years of service, he would be permitted to marry Rachel also. The situation could have easily resulted in quite a row had Jacob been of a more volatile disposition, but being a gentle man, and quite determined to have Rachel as his wife, he obligated himself to another seven years.

As one might expect, the marriage was less than perfect for Leah. It was no secret that Jacob's heart belonged to Rachel, and God compensated by allowing Leah to bear children, while Rachel remained barren. After the birth of Leah's fourth son, Rachel became so envious that she gave her maid, Bilhah, to Jacob, and Bilhah bore him two sons. Not to be outdone, Leah presented Jacob with her maid, Zilpah, and she bore him two more sons. Only after Jacob had fathered eleven children (six sons and one daughter by Leah, two sons by Bilhah and two sons by Zilpah) did God heal Rachel's barrenness, allowing her to give birth to a son named Joseph.

Following is a list of Jacob's thirteen children in birth order according to their birth mothers.

LEAH -   Reuben
            Simeon
            Levi
            Judah

BILHAH -   Dan
(Rachel's maid) Naphtali

ZILPAH -	Gad
(Leah's maid)	Asher
LEAH -	Issachar
	Zebulun
	Dinah
RACHEL -	Joseph
	Benjamin

At the completion of fourteen years of servitude, Jacob desired to return home, but Laban, recognizing the fact that God's blessing was upon Jacob, pleaded with him to remain. *"I have divined that the LORD has blessed me on your account. Name me your wages, and I will give it to you"* (Genesis 30:27–28). Jacob agreed to stay on one condition—that he be permitted to acquire a flock of his own by keeping all of the speckled, spotted, and black offspring for himself. Laban consented, and Jacob remained an additional six years. During those years, God blessed Jacob by causing the strongest of Laban's flocks to reproduce spotted and speckled offspring, which resulted in Jacob's herd growing steadily stronger, while Laban's declined. Consequently, their relationship became strained and God told Jacob, it was time to go home: *"I am the God of Bethel, where you anointed a pillar, where you made a vow to Me; now arise, leave this land and return to the land of your birth"* (Genesis. 31:13).

Fearing that Laban might take his wives and children from him, Jacob secretly gathered his family and livestock and left for Canaan. Laban assembled men and chased after them. Overtaking them, he confronted Jacob, but Jacob held his ground, giving Laban a brief synopsis of the past twenty years: *"These twenty years I have been in your house; I served you fourteen years for your two daughters, and six years for your flock, and you changed my wages ten times. If the God of my father, the God of Abraham, and the fear of Isaac had not been for me, surely now you would have sent me away empty-handed. God has seen my affliction and the toil of my hands, so He rendered judgment last night"* (Genesis 31:41–42). Realizing that he was defeated, Laban gave up. *"The daughters are my daughters, and the children are my children, and the flocks are my flocks, and all that you see is mine. But what can I do this day to these my daughters or to their children whom they have borne? So now come, let us make a covenant, you and I, and let it be a witness between you and me"* (Genesis 31:43–44).

Scripture states that Jacob and Laban cut a covenant (*karath b'rith*), which means that an animal was sacrificed, cut in two, and they walked between the pieces of flesh. Following this ritual, they shared a covenant meal, pledged a vow, and assembled a pile of stones to serve as a sign and memorial of their covenant. They named the heap of stones *Galeed* and *Mizpah* meaning *watchtower*. And they vowed, *"I will not pass by this heap to you for harm, and you will not pass by this heap and this pillar to me for harm"* (Genesis 31:52). Laban then returned to his land and Jacob resumed his journey.

Continuing on, he encountered another obstacle. Jacob's entourage had to pass through the land of his brother, Esau, to reach Canaan. He had no way of knowing if the past twenty years had mellowed Esau, or if he would be placing his entire family in harm's way. Therefore, he sent messengers ahead to speak with Esau and assess the situation. The messengers reported that Esau was coming to meet Jacob with four hundred men. Unsure of how to interpret this response, Jacob cried out to God, "*O God of my father Abraham and God of my father Isaac, O LORD, who didst say to me, 'Return to your country and to your relatives, and I will prosper you,' I am unworthy of all the lovingkindness and of all the faithfulness which Thou hast shown to Thy servant; for with my staff only I crossed this Jordan, and now I have become two companies. Deliver me, I pray, from the hand of my brother, from the hand of Esau; for I fear him, lest he come and attack me, the mothers with the children. For Thou didst say 'I will surely prosper you, and make your descendants as the sand of the sea which cannot be numbered for multitude'*" (Genesis 32:9–12).

God answered Jacob's prayer by instructing him to send gifts to Esau. After making a selection from his herd, Jacob quickly sent three servants ahead to present these animals. Each servant was instructed to offer his gift to Esau, saying, "*These belong to your servant Jacob; it is a present sent to my lord Esau, and behold, he also is behind us*" (Genesis 32:18). As the groups traveled on ahead, Jacob remained behind in camp. That night God visited him, and informed him that his name was going to be changed from Jacob to Israel, meaning "He who strives with God."

The next morning, Jacob awoke to see Esau's approaching army. Was this to be a joyful reunion, or a bloody massacre? Since he had no way of knowing, he separated his family into three groups, placing the two maids and their children first, Leah and her children second, and his beloved Rachael and Joseph in the rear. Then positioning himself in the forefront, Jacob went to meet Esau. He need not have feared for God's plan worked beautifully. When Esau saw Jacob, he *"ran to meet him and embraced him and fell on his neck and kissed him and they wept"* (Genesis 33:4). Hence, Jacob passed safely through the land of Esau, continuing toward home.

After arriving in Canaan, Jacob remembered the vow which he had made twenty years earlier at Bethel. Certainly God had provided for his needs, abundantly prospered him, and paved the way for his safe return to Isaac. Therefore honoring his pledge, Jacob erected an altar and named it "El-Elohe-Israel" meaning, "God, the God of Israel." No longer was God merely the God of Abraham and Isaac, for now He had become the God of Jacob as well, and this altar evidenced their internal Covenant relationship.

Not long after settling in Canaan, Jacob's only daughter, Dinah, was sexually molested by a Hivite prince named Shechem. It seems that Shechem was ignorant of the fact that rape is a despicable act, for afterwards, he took his father, Hamor, and foolishly went to Jacob's home. While Shechem was busy declaring his love for Dinah and requesting her hand in marriage, Hamor took notice of Jacob's obvious wealth and offered a suggestion. "Let the sons of Jacob intermarry with the daughters of the Hivites," he proposed. "Absolutely not!" responded Jacob's sons. They hastened to explain that Dinah could never be given to an uncircumcised male, nor would they consider intermarriage with the Hivites unless every Hivite was circumcised. Shechem and Hamor were not discouraged. Eagerly they carried this message back to the men of their city, and by pointing out the financial benefits of intermarriage with Jacob's sons, they easily convinced the Hivite men that circumcision was a small price to pay for such a lucrative arrangement.

On the third day after their circumcisions, while the Hivite men were recuperating, Dinah's older brothers, Simeon and Levi, went into the city and executed revenge for the crime against their sister. They killed every male, took their wives and children, and looted their wealth. When Jacob heard about it, he was angry. *"You have brought trouble on me, by making me odious among the inhabitants of the land, among the Canaanites and the Perizzites,"* he screamed. *"My men being few in number, they will gather together against me and attack me and I shall be destroyed, I and my household"* (Genesis 34:30). The threat of impending danger caused Jacob to momentarily forget the protection of God's Covenant promise. But God reminded him by jolting him back to reality with these instructions, *"Arise, go up to Bethel, and live there; and make an altar there to God, who appeared to you when you fled from your brother Esau"* (Genesis 35:1). Jacob and his family moved to Bethel, and there God appeared to him and changed his name from Jacob to Israel. He said, *"Your name is Jacob; you shall no longer be called Jacob, but Israel shall be your name. I am God Almighty, be fruitful and multiply; a nation and a company of nations shall come from you, and kings shall come forth from you. And the land which I gave to Abraham and Isaac, I will give it to you, and I will give the land to your descendants after you* (Genesis 35:10–12). At this point in Jacob's life, Rachel died giving birth to his twelfth son, Benjamin.

Jacob summed up his life with these words, *"I will make an altar there to God who answered me in the day of my distress, and has been with me wherever I have gone"* (Genesis

35:3). Life for Jacob was never a bed of roses. He was hated by his brother, and cheated by his uncle. Having two wives, two concubines, and thirteen children made his life far from tranquil. He experienced the ups and downs, and unexpected twists and turns that make their way into all of our lives, yet Jacob knew what it meant to be a part of God's Covenant. He remained confident that no matter where he was, or what was happening in his life, he could rely upon God to keep His Covenant promises. It is a truth we do well to remember.

Did you notice that when Jacob saw Esau's army approaching, he spoke to God about the Covenant? He said, "God, you promised to prosper me and make my seed as numerous as the sand of the sea which cannot be numbered." Why would he do that?

Was he afraid that God had forgotten? Of course not! In the face of danger, Jacob was strengthened by reminding himself that God is a Covenant-keeping God. He sets an excellent example for us. Most of us will never face an oncoming army, but all of us will encounter our share of difficulties. During those trying times, we find strength in the fact that God has not changed, and His promises are as true for us today as they were for Jacob. God promised that under no circumstances would He ever leave or forsake those who are in Covenant with Him. He has promised to love, protect, guide, heal, strengthen, and meet all the needs of those who belong to Him. By the way, the meaning of that Greek word *all* is ALL.

Are you fearful today? If God is your Covenant Partner, you needn't be. Your life is in His hands and He has promised to take care of you. Listen to what David said as he hid and watched Saul's army approaching. *"The Lord is my light and my salvation; whom shall I fear? The Lord is the defense of my life; whom shall I dread? When evildoers came upon me to devour my flesh, my adversaries and my enemies, they stumbled and fell. Though a host encamp against me, my heart will not fear; though war arise against me, in spite of this I shall be confident"* (Psalm 27:1–3). David knew what it meant to be God's Covenant partner. How about you? Do you have fears that leave you tossing and turning, losing sleep at night? If you are in Covenant with God, He is well aware of the situation and can be trusted. He has promised to be with you, and to meet all of your needs so you needn't live in fear.

Jacob witnessed the faith of Isaac and no doubt listened to Abraham tell and retell the story of how God cut Covenant with him, but that was not enough. Realizing that he could not survive on the faith of his father or grandfather, he sought his own relationship with God. Likewise, you and I cannot survive on the faith of a parent, grandparent, spouse, pastor, priest, or teacher. God said that Christianity is a personal, intimate Covenant relationship, a one-on-one with God. Jacob understood this. His desire for a personal relationship with God prompted his conditional vow at Bethel, where he vowed that *if* God would be with him, and *if* God would provide for him, and *if* God would then take him safely back to his father, *then* he would worship Him. It was a conditional vow, but not a ploy. Jacob was not smugly demanding that God prove Himself. He was giving his word. He was promising to surrender all that he was, and all that he had upon the assurance that God would be his God, as well as the God of Abraham and Isaac. He was searching with all of his heart, therefore God honored his request.

This is nice story with a happy ending, but does it have anything to do with our lives today? If we ask, does God reveal Himself to us? Yes, of course, He does.

Keeping in mind that He does not change, His words still ring true: *"You will seek Me and find Me, when you search for Me with all your heart* (Jeremiah 29:13). Only God knows the motivation of our heart. It is possible for us to acquire biblical knowledge and not know God. There are individuals whose biblical knowledge prompts stimulating conversations and endless debates. However, biblical knowledge does not guarantee a relationship. God says that He is only found by the individual who searches with his heart. *"I love those who love Me; and those who diligently seek Me will find Me,"* He promises. (Proverbs 8:17).

Back in the 1970's when the charismatic movement was sweeping across the nation, there were many wonderful books describing how God had revealed Himself to someone who was seeking Him. *The Cross and the Switchblade* by David Wilkerson, and *They Speak with Other Tongues* by John Sherrill are among my favorites. But God used *A New Song* by Pat Boone to reveal Himself to a young man who was searching.

Late one evening, Dan sat in his favorite chair and began reading *A New Song*. It was quite late when he finished the last page and closing his eyes he prayed, "God, if this is real, give me a sign." Instantly, a loud popping sound emanated from the television, and the screen went blank. Dan leaped from his chair in disbelief and stared at the sizzling set. After a few seconds, regaining composure, he bravely unplugged the set, and went to bed.

The next morning with a sheepish grin, he asked his wife to call a repairman, "Our television is not working," was all he said, but she knew by the look on his face that there was more to the story. That afternoon, the repairman arrived, pulled the set away from the wall, and removed the back panel. Momentarily, she heard him grumble in disgust, "Somebody's been messing with your set. The wires are crossed back here." Sure enough, two incorrectly attached wires were forming a cross on the back of the television.

That evening when Dan explained the rest of the story, he and his wife laughed and praised God together. How very much like our loving, Covenant-keeping God to answer the sincere cry of Dan's heart by forming a wire cross on the back of his television set.

Perhaps you can relate to Dan's question. You may be reading this book and wondering, *"Can this be true?"* If you are, and if you truly want to know God, talk to Him. He will customize a reply just for you. You will have no doubt that He exists, that He loves you, and that His desire is for you to walk with Him. God never violates the free will He has given us, but when we take that first step in His direction, we find Him waiting with open arms.

Chapter 10

WALKING IN GOD'S COVENANT

(Joseph)

We have seen that God made the Covenant promise to Adam and Eve, preserved it through Noah, cut it in blood with Abraham, swore an oath to Isaac, and confirmed it to Jacob. Link by link, generation to generation, His Covenant chain exclusively passed from one chosen individual to another. However, with the birth of Jacob's twelve sons, things were destined for change. The Messiah would come from the lineage of Jacob's son Judah, but all of his sons would have a part to play in God's plan. And Joseph, "*the one distinguished among his brothers,*" starred in a leading role.

Long before Joseph's birth, the stage was set with deceit, contention, and jealousy. Jacob loved Rachel, but was tricked into marrying Leah. When he wound up married to both sisters, the discord in his household began. Leah was jealous of Jacob's love for Rachel, and Rachel was envious because she remained barren while Leah gave birth to sons. Adding more fuel to the smoldering coals of discontent, both Leah and Rachel gave their maids to Jacob. This resulted in the birth of four more sons. By the time Joseph arrived, Jacob had already fathered ten sons and one daughter. It is probably safe to assume that Rachel and Jacob were the only ones rejoicing over the birth of Joseph.

Rachel was the love of Jacob's life, so it is understandable that her son would be his favorite. However, it was a situation which nearly cost Joseph his life. The normal sibling rivalry expected in a household of thirteen children was intensified by the fact that Jacob *"loved Joseph more than all his sons,"* and showed it (Genesis 37:3). As a sign of is affection, Jacob gave seventeen-year-old Joseph a beautiful, multi-colored tunic, and his brothers took offense. Seeing him in the tunic was a painful reminder that he was their father's favorite. Joseph made matters worse by being the proverbial younger brother who took great pleasure in snitching on his older siblings. Consequently, his brothers *"hated him and could not speak to him on friendly terms"* (Genesis 37:4).

Things progressed from bad to worse when God gave Joseph two prophetic dreams. In the first dream, he and his brothers were binding sheaves in a field, and his sheaf rose up and stood erect, while his brothers' sheaves bowed down to it (Genesis 37:5–7). In the second dream, the sun, the moon, and eleven stars bowed down before Joseph (Genesis 37:9–11). It would have been wise for Joseph to have kept these dreams to himself. Instead, he insisted upon telling his brothers, causing their relationship to become even more strained. They nicknamed him "The Dreamer," and *"hated him even more for his dreams,"* (Genesis 37:8). When Jacob heard about the dreams, he reprimanded Joseph saying, *"What is this dream that you have had? Shall I and your mother and your brothers actually come to bow ourselves down before you to the ground?"* (Genesis 37:10). But remembering his own divine encounter, Jacob secretly acknowledged the possibility that these were prophetic dreams coming from God. (Genesis 37:11).

The unfolding of God's plan and the fulfillment of these prophetic dreams began one ordinary day, when Joseph was sent to check on his brothers who were tending the flock some distance away. It was something which he routinely did. However, on this day as his brothers saw him approaching with his beautiful robe fluttering in the breeze, their jealousy gave rise to a plan to rid themselves of 'The Dreamer' forever. "Let's kill him," Judah offered. "No," argued Rubin, "we cannot shed our brother's blood. Let's throw him in this pit." Seizing Joseph, they stripped off his robe and forced him down into a deep pit. He pleaded, but their hardened hearts remained untouched by his cries, until an approaching caravan provided a solution to their dilemma (Genesis 37:25, 42:21). "Let's sell him to the Ishmaelites," Judah suggested. Quickly hoisting him out of the pit, they sold Joseph for twenty shekels of silver. Before returning home, his brothers splattered Joseph's beautiful robe with animal blood, making it appear as if he had been devoured by a wild beast. Then feigning sorrow, they presented the blood-soaked robe to Jacob, allowing him to draw his own conclusions. As one might expect, Jacob was beyond consolation. Rachel was dead, and now his favorite son was gone.

"*Surely I will go down to Sheol in mourning for my son,*" he lamented (Genesis 37:35).

The stage was now set for Act II of God's plan. While Jacob mourned, Joseph was taken to Egypt and sold as a slave to an officer named Potiphar. In a short time, Potiphar noticed that the Lord was with Joseph, causing "*all that he did to prosper in his hand*" (Genesis 39:2–3). Being a wise man, Potiphar took advantage of this unique situation and made Joseph overseer of all he owned. "*The Lord blessed the Egyptian's house on account of Joseph*" (Genesis 39:5).

Things went well for Joseph until he matured and grew more handsome. Then lust reared its ugly head in the form of Potiphar's wife. She wanted Joseph and was determined to have him. Day after day she sought opportunities to be near him, to touch him, to catch his eye, and with a concupiscent grin to whisper, "Lie with me." Although her enticement was relentless, Joseph managed to keep her at bay. Attempting to reason with her, he explained, "*My master does not concern himself with anything in the house, and he has put all that he owns in my charge. There is no one greater in this house than I, and he has withheld nothing from me except you, because you are his wife. How then could I do this great evil, and sin against God?*" (Genesis 39:8–9). Joseph discovered that reasoning with the spirit of lust is like trying to hold back the wind. Mrs. Potiphar would not be denied. She was the personification of the adulterous woman described in Proverbs 5:3: "*The lips of an adulteress drip honey, and smoother than oil is her speech; but in the end she is bitter as wormwood.*"

One day while Potiphar was away, Mrs. Potiphar determined to conquer Joseph. She dismissed the servants, slipped into her most provocative gown, lavishly applied her most sensual perfume, and set out to find him. Seeing him standing at a distance with his back toward her, she seductively moistened her lips and slithered up from behind, catching him completely off guard. *"Lie with me,"* she hissed. Joseph felt simultaneously trapped and enticed as her arms clutched at his body and her essence overtook him. *"Lie with me,"* she whispered again. As he felt himself responding to the magnetism of her embrace, Joseph became terrified. "NO!" he bellowed. In one swift, twisting motion, he freed himself from her arms, and ran, leaving the screaming Mrs. Potiphar clutching his garment. Joseph most likely ran like he had never run before, stopping only when his legs refused to carry him another step. Then collapsing into a heap, he must have shuddered at his narrow escape, and admitted to himself that something had to change. Something had to be done to stop this lustful, adulterous woman. But what?

Meanwhile back at the house, the rejected and angry Mrs. Potiphar had come to the same conclusion. Never again would she be scorned by this man. Twisting and tearing his garment, she devised a wicked, revengeful plan. For hours she waited for Potiphar's return, rehearsing the wretched details over and over again in her mind, until she almost believed them herself. Upon hearing Potiphar's approaching footsteps, she briskly rubbed her eyes to make it appear as if she had been crying. Then running to meet him, she hysterically screamed, *"The Hebrew slave, whom you brought to us, came in to make sport of me; and it happened as I raised my voice and screamed, that he left his garment beside me and fled outside"* (Genesis 39:17–18). As a result of her wantonness and lies, Joseph was thrown into prison, setting the stage for Act III of God's plan.

He was unjustly imprisoned, yet *"the Lord was with Joseph and extended kindness to him and gave him favor in the sight of the chief jailer"* who promptly put him in charge of the other prisoners (Genesis 39:21). It so happened that Pharaoh's cup bearer and baker were also imprisoned. One night, they both had disturbing dreams, and God gave Joseph the interpretations. To the chief cup bearer he said, *"Within three more days Pharaoh will lift up your head and restore you to your office . . . keep me in mind when it goes well with you, and please do me a kindness by mentioning me to Pharaoh, and get me out of this house* (Genesis 40:13-14). Unfortunately, the interpretation for the baker was not as upbeat, and Joseph had the unpleasant task of informing him that within three days he would be killed (Genesis 40:19). The events unfolded just as Joseph had predicted, but once freed, the cup bearer forgot about his promise.

Two years later, while Joseph was still imprisoned, Pharaoh had two dreams which none of the wise men of Egypt were able to interpret. It was then that the cup bearer remembered his promise to Joseph, and told Pharaoh about the imprisoned Hebrew. Immediately, Joseph was released from jail and summoned to interpret Pharaoh's dreams. He said to Pharaoh, *"God has told Pharaoh what He is about to do"* (Genesis 41:25). *"Behold, seven years of great abundance are coming in all the land of Egypt; and after them seven years of famine will come, and all the abundance will be forgotten in the land of Egypt; and the famine will ravage the land. So the abundance will be unknown in the land because of that subsequent famine; for it will be very severe* (Genesis 41:25-32).

Humbly, Joseph offered a solution. "*Let Pharaoh look for a man discerning and wise, and set him over the land of Egypt. Let Pharaoh take action to appoint overseers in charge of the land, and let him exact a fifth of the produce of the land of Egypt in the seven years of abundance. Then let them gather all the food of these good years that are coming, and store up the grain for food in the cities under Pharaoh's authority, and let them guard it. And let the food become as a reserve for the land for the seven years of famine which will occur in the land of Egypt, so that the land may not perish during the famine* (Genesis 41:33–37).

This seemed like an excellent suggestion, and since Joseph appeared to be the wisest man in all of Egypt, Pharaoh appointed him Overseer. Thirty-year-old Joseph went from prisoner to Overseer of Egypt in a matter of minutes. Pharaoh took off his signet ring and placed it on Joseph's finger. He clothed him in the finest linen, placed a gold necklace around his neck, and gave him a wife by the name of Asenath. Wherever Joseph went, people bowed before him. God gave him wisdom and ability beyond his years and experience, so that Egypt was well prepared for the famine. There was such an abundance of grain stored in Egypt that even those living outside the city came to purchase grain from Joseph.

Back in Canaan, Joseph's family suffered the effects of the famine for two years. Finally, Jacob said to his sons, "Why are you standing around looking at one another, when there is food available in Egypt? Go down and buy some grain." Ten of Joseph's brothers left for Egypt, while Benjamin, the youngest, remained with Jacob.

The Forgotten Covenant

When Joseph saw his brothers, he immediately recognized them, although they did not know him. Seeing them bow before him surely caused Joseph to recall the dreams God had given him as a youth. He wanted to tell them who he was, and had so many questions he wanted to ask: Was his father still living? Where was Benjamin? Did they have wives and children of their own? Joseph could not bear the thought of their leaving, so he devised a plan to delay their departure. Much to their surprise, he accused them of being spies. *"You have come to look at the undefended parts of our land,"* he bellowed (Genesis 42:9). Then he ordered them thrown into prison for three days, while he contrived a scheme to insure their return to Egypt. On the third day as they were being released, he said to them, *"If you are honest men, let one of your brothers be confined in your prison; but as for the rest of you, go carry grain for the famine of your households, and bring your youngest brother to me, so your words may be verified, and you will not die"* (Genesis 42:19–20). It was decided that Simeon would remain, while the others sorrowfully returned to Jacob.

In time, their supply of grain became depleted and Joseph's brothers were faced with a return trip to Egypt. However, Jacob forbid them to take Benjamin. *"You have bereaved me of my children: Joseph is no more, and Simeon is no more, and you would take Benjamin; all of these things are against me,"* he lamented (Genesis 42:36). But Judah reminded him of Joseph's solemn warning, not to return without Benjamin, and pledging his life, he entreated Jacob, *"Send the lad with me, and we will arise and go, that we may live and not die, we as well as you and our little ones. I myself will be surety for him; you may hold me responsible for him. If I do not bring him back to you and set him before you, then let me bear the blame before you forever"* (Genesis 43:8–9). Reluctantly, Jacob agreed.

The moment Joseph saw Benjamin, he was overcome with such emotion that he could scarcely withhold the sobs that welled up inside. Quickly he excused himself, seeking the privacy of his own chambers. When he finally regained composure, he returned to share a meal with his brothers. Afterwards, as they were preparing to leave, Joseph instructed his steward to place his own silver cup in Benjamin's bag. This was another ploy to insure their return. They had scarcely gotten out of the city, when Joseph sent his steward to overtake them and accuse them of stealing the silver cup. They thought it such an absurd accusation that they said to the steward, "If you find the cup in any of our bags, the one who took it will die and the rest of us will be your slaves."

"That won't be necessary," the steward replied. "The one who has the cup will be my slave, and the rest of you shall be innocent." They were aghast when the silver cup was discovered in Benjamin's sack.

Distraught, they returned to Egypt and fell prostrate before Joseph. He assured them that with the exception of Benjamin, they were free to leave. Judah was horrified. Bowing before Joseph, he begged to be permitted to take Benjamin's place.

"Our elderly father will die if we return without Benjamin," he sobbed. Hearing Judah plead for his brother's life was more than Joseph could bear. Abruptly, he ordered everyone except his brothers to leave the room. Then weeping so loudly that he could be heard by the Egyptians outside, he cried, *"I am Joseph! Is my father still alive?"* His brothers were speechless. *"Please come closer to me."* he said. *"I am your brother, Joseph, whom you sold into Egypt. And now do not be grieved or angry with yourselves because you sold me here; for God sent me before you to preserve life. For the famine as been in the land these two years; and there are still five years in which there will be neither plowing nor harvesting. And God sent me before you to preserve for you a remnant in the earth, and to keep you alive by a great deliverance. Now, therefore, it was not you who sent me here, but God"* (Genesis 45:3–8).

With Pharaoh's permission, Joseph instructed his brothers to return to Jacob, gather their families, and move to Egypt. *"I will give you the best of the land of Egypt, and you shall eat the fat of the land,"* Pharaoh promised them (Genesis 45:18). When Jacob's sons returned with the news that Joseph was alive and that he was the Overseer of Egypt, Jacob was overcome with joy. Immediately he went to Beersheba to offer sacrifices of thanksgiving. There God spoke to him in a vision saying, *"Do not be afraid to go down to Egypt, for I will make you a great nation there. I will go down with you to Egypt, and I will also surely bring you up again; and Joseph will close your eyes"* (Genesis 46:3–4). Therefore, Jacob and his family, totaling sixty-six men plus their wives and children, made their way to Egypt, settling in the best of the land.

Seventeen years later, while still living in Egypt, Jacob died. Although Joseph had long ago forgiven his brothers, after Jacob's death, they grew concerned, fearing that with their father gone, Joseph might feel free to execute revenge upon them. So they sent a message to him saying, *"Your father charged before he died, saying, Thus you shall say to Joseph, 'Please forgive, I beg you, the transgression of your brothers and their sin, for they did you wrong. And now, please forgive the transgression of the servants of the God of your father'"* (Genesis 50:16–17). Joseph wept. In the throes of emotion, he tried again to make them understand that he did not hold them responsible for what had happened. *"Do not be afraid, for am I in God's place?"* he said. *"And as for you, you meant evil against me, but God meant it for good in order to bring about this present result, to preserve many people alive. So therefore, do not be afraid; I will provide for you and your little ones"* (Genesis 50:20–21). And he did.

Perhaps you are wondering how Joseph could forgive his brothers. His childhood was marred by their jealousy and hatred. They were unkind to him, rejected him, planned to kill him, and then sold him. He could have rationalized that they were indirectly responsible for his being imprisoned. Yet, Joseph felt only love for his brothers, and was able to forgive them because he lived his life in the reality of Romans 8:28. He knew that *"God causes all things to work together for good, to those who love God, to those who are called according to His purpose."* He was certain that God was directing his life. As a youth, feeling the sting of jealousy and rejection, God had comforted him with prophetic dreams. When his brothers wanted to kill him, it was God who prevented it, causing him to be placed in a pit until he could be safely sold to the passing caravan.

God's presence in Joseph's life was so obvious that Potiphar saw it and trusted him with all he owned. The jailer recognized it, and felt comfortable putting Joseph in charge of the other prisoners. God interpreted the dreams of the baker, the cup bearer, and Pharaoh to place Joseph where He wanted him to be, in a position of power in Egypt. It is true that Joseph endured difficult times, yet he never complained, because he understood that all things, even the injustices, were orchestrated by God and filtered through His fingers of love. Joseph knew that underlying every situation was God's divine purpose.

The story of Joseph is one to remember, whenever we are hurt or treated unjustly. Understanding that God causes all things, even the cruel and unjust things, to work together for good to those who love Him is an important aspect of walking in Covenant with Him. As Christians, we maintain a proper perspective by keeping our focus upon God, rather than on the actions of those around us. Joseph was hated, rejected, sold, and victimized. Yet, his total surrender to the will of God lifted him above the usual human response of retaliation. Since God has not changed, a relationship with Him will do the same for you and me. When we have been hurt and our flesh is screaming for revenge, if we choose instead to "put on" the robe of our Covenant Partner, surrendering ourselves anew to God's will, He meets us at the point of our human weakness and fills us with His strength. It is a choice, as illustrated in the following story.

Jody and Bert worked for an advertising firm. Jody was a tall, slender, attractive, bubbly secretary. Bert was a loud, overweight artist who spoke with a cowboy drawl that made Jody's skin crawl. Each morning as part of her duties, Jody purchased and served coffee to the thirty men in her office. She didn't mind serving the others, but very much resented having to wait on Bert. They shared a mutual dislike.

Every morning Bert greeted her with the same demeaning command, "Smile, Jody." *I'm not smiling because the sight of you makes me sick*, she wanted to say, but didn't. She felt that Bert took great pleasure in belittling and using her. Like clockwork the same ritual was re-enacted every day. Instead of ordering two cups of coffee, Bert waited until Jody purchased and delivered all thirty cups, then sent her scurrying back to the cafeteria to buy him a second. *He looks as if he's devoured seconds of everything his entire life*, Jody mused, as she stomped off to the cafeteria.

Then something happened which changed their relationship. Jody became a born-again Christian and discovered that Jesus expected her to love her enemies and to pray for those who despitefully used her. "God, I cannot love him," she cried, "but I can pray for him." So each morning, prior to Bert's arrival, Jody prayed for him. Before he could demand a smile, she willed her facial muscles to relax into the biggest possible grin. "Well, that's more like it, little lady," he chided, acknowledging her effort. *God, I feel like a hypocrite*, Jody silently protested.

"Just do it," God's internal voice whispered. When it was time to take Bert's coffee order, she forced another smile and in a chipper voice suggested, "How about two cups?"

"Good idea, little lady," Bert drawled, as he tossed another coin in her direction. "Here's another ten cents; get yourself a cup too."

As Jody continued to obey God's Word and pray daily for Bert, he became less irritating. The edge began to disappear from their relationship and in time, they became friends. Eventually, Bert left the firm and Jody never saw him again. Several years later, a mutual friend met Bert and he inquired about Jody. "You know," he said, "at first, I didn't like her at all. I don't know what happened, but she turned out to be a mighty special little gal."

What Bert didn't realize was that he had experienced God's miracle-working power. At the fusion of Jody's obedience and God's faithfulness, there was a supernatural explosion of power which changed their relationship. This is just one of the many reasons why every Christian needs to have an understanding of God's Covenant.

Knowing that there is eternal life waiting after death for God's Covenant partners is wonderful, but it is only a part of His provision. He also promises an abundant life beginning here and now for all those who belong to Him. It isn't a life free of difficulties, but rather a life filled with the presence and power of God. The enemy would like to keep believers ignorant in this regard, because he knows that without the undergirding of God's strength, Christians are vulnerable. In moments of weakness, we can be unforgiving, lustful, prideful, and greedy. Yet when we understand that Christianity is a Covenant, and we live in the reality of it, our Covenant Partner provides all the strength, wisdom, and protection we need. Consequently, the enemy is doomed, and our lives are changed.

Keeping in mind that these Old Testament events are recorded for our instruction, we would be remiss if we did not learn something from Joseph's experience with Potiphar's wife. Let's briefly review the story. Jealousy and rejection were the taskmasters that shaped Joseph's early years. Had he not known God, he could have easily become a hard, cynical individual, but Joseph was a sensitive man. Having endured more than his share of rejection, he was unwilling to inflict such pain on anyone else, not even Potiphar's adulterous wife. He initially tried to curtail her advances by reasoning with her, explaining that she was off limits, not only because she was Potiphar's wife, but because of his relationship with God. Remember, he posed the question, *"How could I do this great evil and sin against God?"* (Genesis 39:9).

Joseph considered adultery to be more than a betrayal of Potiphar's trust. It was a betrayal of his relationship with God. He had learned how to live and move and have his being in God, regardless of the circumstances in which he found himself. Mrs. Potiphar, however, had no such convictions. She remained persistent in her seduction, knowing that it was only a matter of time before Joseph weakened. Joseph, being well aware of his weakness, relied upon God's strength. He did not have the luxury of reading God's instructions regarding the adulterous woman given in Proverbs 5:8, *"Keep your way far from her, and do not go near the door of her house"*, so God taught him.

Unexpectedly finding himself locked in Mrs. Potiphar's arms, reeling from the intoxication of her perfume, and feeling his body involuntarily respond to the electricity of her embrace, Joseph *ran*. God gave him the supernatural strength and wisdom to remove himself from the temptation. He does the same for His Covenant partners today.

Just for a moment, let's consider what might have happened had Joseph not run, if he had instead given in to the temptation and committed adultery. It is quite likely that Potiphar would have had Joseph killed, and his death would have had a devastating domino effect. He would not have been there to interpret Pharaoh's dreams, Egypt would have been unprepared for the famine, thousands, including

Joseph's family, would have lost their lives, and God's Covenant chain would have been needlessly broken.

Applying this to our lives today, we would have to conclude that thousands would probably not die if you or I failed in the area of morality. Yet God's Word clearly states that the wages of sin is death (Romans 6:23). It could be the death of a marriage, a relationship, a home, a job, trust, and most certainly peace of mind. The things which matter the most are fragile and can be altered or destroyed by one selfish act of betrayal. Knowing this, God made a promise to His Covenant partners. He said, *"No temptation has overtaken you but such as is common to man; and God is faithful, who will not allow you to be tempted beyond what you are able, but with the temptation will provide the way of escape also, that you may be able to endure it"* (1 Corinthians 10:13). Joseph's story is one to remember whenever we find ourselves looking into the eyes of that beguiling spirit of immorality. When it happens, and *it will happen*, we do well to remember God's words and Joseph's example. *"Keep your way far from her"* and if she shows up unexpectedly, *run!* Too many slip into immorality, because they foolishly delude themselves into thinking that they can handle it. Unlike Joseph, they depend upon their own strength, rather than relying upon the strength of their Covenant Partner. "I can handle this," they insist. "It is just a harmless flirtation." Not so, God warns: *"Let him who thinks he stands take heed, lest he fall"* (1 Corinthians 10:12). Christians finding themselves in a similar situation are wise to heed God's warning and to follow Joseph's example. *Run!*

Because Joseph was faithful, God placed him in a position of power in Egypt, and used him to preserve the Covenant bloodline. I am quite sure that Joseph never planned on moving to Egypt. He certainly never imagined that he would spend years in prison for a crime he did not commit, and then become Overseer of Egypt. God orchestrated Joseph's life, and He continues to do so for all those who belong to Him. If you want to know God and walk in this Covenant relationship with Him, accept His invitation. Surrender yourself to Him by receiving Jesus as your personal Lord and Savior, and give Him complete control of your life. Jesus said, *"I came that they might have life, and might have it abundantly"* (John 10:10). It is time to move out of the driver's seat and start experiencing the journey He has prepared for you.

Chapter 11

THE ISRAELITES ENTER GOD'S COVENANT

(The Israelites)

The sons of Jacob lived, prospered, and multiplied in Egypt for over seventy years. After the deaths of Joseph and the reigning Pharaoh, things changed. The new Pharaoh knew nothing about Joseph, nor how these Hebrews had come to be living in the land of Goshen. *"In the event of war, they might join themselves to those who hate us and fight against us,"* he surmised (Exodus 1:10). Therefore, he enslaved them, and they remained slaves in Egypt for four hundred years, just as God had prophesied to Abraham. However, God was well aware of their situation, and was raising up a deliverer long before they asked for His help.

It seemed to Pharaoh that the more he afflicted the Israelites, *"the more they multiplied and spread out"* (Exodus 1:12). So he issued a decree, saying, *"Every son who is born you are to cast into the Nile, and every daughter you are to* keep alive." (Exodus 1:22). At this time, a descendant of Jacob's son Levi gave birth to a baby boy, and hid the child for three months. When it was no longer possible to conceal him, she placed him in a wicker basket covered with tar and pitch, and set him among the reeds on the bank of the Nile. From a distance, his older sister, Miriam, watched to see what would happen.

The baby began to cry, as the daughter of Pharaoh came to bathe in the river. She felt sorry for the infant and decided to take him to be her son. Miriam, who had been watching from a distance, approached Pharaoh's daughter, asking, *"Shall I go and call a nurse for you from the Hebrew women, that she may nurse the child for you?"* (Exodus 1:7). When she agreed, Miriam brought the child's mother to nurse him. Moses was raised as the son of Pharaoh's daughter, but was nursed by his biological mother.

As an adult, Moses saw a Hebrew slave being beaten by an Egyptian guard, and he responded by killing the guard. This incident forced him to flee for his life, and God directed him to the land of Midian, where he met a priest named Jethro. Jethro gave his daughter, Zipporah, to be Moses' wife, and she bore him a son. Life remained peaceful for him, until the time came for God to deliver His people from bondage.

One day as Moses was pasturing Jethro's flock, God spoke to him from a burning bush, saying, *"I am the God of your father, the God of Abraham, the God of Isaac, and the God of Jacob* (Exodus 3:6). *I have surely seen the affliction of My people who are in Egypt, and have given heed to their cry because of their taskmasters, for I am aware of their suffer-*

The Israelites Enter God's Covenant

ings. *So I have come down to deliver them from the power of the Egyptians, and to bring them up from that land to a good and spacious land, to a land flowing with milk and honey* (Exodus 3:7–8). *". . . Therefore, come now, and I will send you to Pharaoh, so that you may bring My people, the sons of Israel, out of Egypt"* (Exodus 3:10).

Moses was reluctant. *"Who am I, that I should go to Pharaoh,"* he asked. But God assured him, *"I will be with you"* (Exodus 3:11–12). Trying to fully prepare himself for the task at hand, Moses asked, *"When the sons of Israel inquire as to who sent me to them, what shall I say?"* *"And God said to Moses, 'I AM WHO I AM, thus you shall say to the sons of Israel, I AM has sent me to you . . . the Lord, the God of your fathers, the God of Abraham, the God of Isaac, and the God of Jacob, has sent me to you. This is My name forever, and this is My memorial name to all generations'"* (Exodus 3:13–15). Moses obeyed.

The Deliverance

The deliverance of the Israelites is a familiar story which has been portrayed in several Hollywood films. Therefore, assuming that you are somewhat familiar with it, let's look closely at how their deliverance related to God's Covenant. Using Moses as His spokesmen, God commanded Pharaoh to let His people go. Each time Pharaoh refused, God struck Egypt with a plague. He turned their waters to blood, sent frogs to invade their land, and caused swarms of gnats to attack them. Their livestock died, boils erupted on their bodies, and their crops were destroyed by hail and locusts. They endured three days of such impermeable darkness that no one dared to venture outside their homes. Still Pharaoh's heart remained hardened. Only a plague of death could force him to release the Israelites.

The Israelites were not affected by the first eight plagues against Egypt, but in order to escape this final plague, they would have to carefully follow God's instructions. Through Moses, God instructed each Hebrew family to kill a one-year-old, unblemished lamb and place the lamb's blood on the doorposts and lintels of their homes. "I am the Lord," He said. *"And the blood shall be a sign for you on the houses where you live and when I see the blood, I will pass over you, and no plague will befall you to destroy you when I strike the land of Egypt"* (Exodus 12:13). That night, the angel of death passed through the land of Egypt, killing the first-born of man and beast in every Egyptian household. The Israelites were passed over because of the blood which was clearly visible on the doorposts and lintels of their homes. They were protected by the blood of the lamb.

In the morning as Egypt mourned its dead, Pharaoh released the Israelites. Leaving en masse with an angel leading them, they traveled until God instructed them to make camp at the Red Sea. Meanwhile, Pharaoh had a change of heart, and furiously assembled his army, setting out to overtake them. With the Red Sea before them and Pharaoh's army in hot pursuit, the Israelites were trapped and frightened. Fixing the blame on Moses, they cried, "How could you do this to us? Did you bring us out into the wilderness to die?" But Moses addressed them with divine confidence,

The Israelites Enter God's Covenant

saying, *"The Lord will fight for you while you keep silent"* (Exodus 14:14). Though the situation appeared hopeless, God was very much in control, carefully orchestrating this scenario for a specific purpose. He said, *"I will harden Pharaoh's heart, and he will chase after them; and I will be honored through Pharaoh and all his army, and the Egyptians will know that I am the Lord"* (Exodus 14:4).

As Pharaoh's army approached, God instructed Moses to lift his staff up over the sea. As he did, the sea divided, enabling the Israelites to pass safely to the other side on dry ground. The angel who had been leading them by a pillar of cloud went behind them, acting as their rear guard. As the last of the Israelites passed safely across, God created confusion among the Egyptians. Causing their chariots to swerve uncontrollably, He let them know that they were encountering His supernatural power. *"Let us flee from Israel, for the Lord is fighting for them against the Egyptians,"* they exclaimed (Exodus 14:25). But it was too late. Instantly, God caused the sea to return to its normal state, drowning Pharaoh and his entire army. On the other side, the Israelites celebrated, singing, dancing and praising God for their miraculous deliverance.

What does this story tell us about God's Covenant? Let's begin by looking closely at the passover. The Israelites were saved from death and set free from Egyptian bondage, because of the blood of the lamb. The passover is a graphic picture of the fulfillment of God's Covenant. As John the Baptist saw Jesus approaching, he said, *"Behold the Lamb of God who takes away the sin of the world!"* (John 1:29). Speaking of the coming Messiah, the prophet Isaiah wrote, *"Like a lamb that is led to slaughter, And like a sheep that is silent before its shearers, So He* [Jesus] *did not open His mouth"* (Isaiah 53:7). Writing to encourage believers who were scattered abroad, Peter wrote, *"You were not redeemed with perishable things like silver or gold from your futile way of life inherited from your forefathers, but with precious blood, as of a lamb unblemished and spotless, the blood of Christ"* (1 Peter 1:18–19). You and I have inherited that futile way of life from our forefathers. Because of what happened in the Garden of Eden, we are born separated from God. We come into this world shaking our little clenched fists in God's face, screaming "I will do as I please." If you doubt this, spend some time observing the behavior of toddlers. As young as six months old, children exhibit evidence of temper and rebellion. Give them a toy that they don't want, and they'll hurl it across the room. Try to feed them something that they don't like, and you could end up wearing it. Deny them anything, and they are likely to throw a temper tantrum. It is the nature of the flesh. The flesh wants to be in control. "Feed me, clothe me, praise me, pamper me, love me," it incessantly demands. The flesh is all about *Me*. And in catering to the insatiable demands of our flesh, we are unwittingly held in bondage. What can set us free? *Nothing* but the blood of the Lamb! Just as the Israelites were set free from their captivity by the blood of the lamb, we are set free from bondage to our flesh and the enemy of our souls by the blood of the Lamb, Jesus Christ.

As the Israelites fled Egypt, anticipating a life of freedom, they faced two powerful enemies. Remembering that these Old Testament accounts have been recorded for our example, let's consider them one at a time.

The Israelites Enter God's Covenant

Israel's first and most obvious enemy was Pharaoh and his army. God had miraculously delivered them and instructed them to make camp at the Red Sea. They probably experienced a gamut of emotions as they sang and danced, but they were certainly not prepared to see Pharaoh again so soon. Looking at this scene in a spiritual sense, we see that as Christians, we will encounter unexpected attacks from Satan, the enemy of our soul. Without warning he will show up, hoping to entrap us. What are we to do? What did Moses do when he saw Pharaoh's army approaching? Moses immediately sought God's help, which is exactly what we are to do. Second Timothy 1:7 tells us that *"God hath not given us a spirit of fear; but of power, and of love, and of a sound mind"* (KJV). It is a given that we have God's love, and that His power is available to us, but long before the enemy shows up, we can prepare for his attack by utilizing our God-given sound mind as a first line of defense. We do this by being brutally honest with ourselves and identifying potential areas of entrapment. Mine will differ from yours, but we all have them, areas where we have repeatedly failed in the past. For instance, if you have a problem with alcohol, you will not watch Monday night football in a sports bar. If you are a shopaholic, you won't exercise by walking in a mall. If you struggle with lust, you will avoid books, movies, and situations which tend to weaken your resolve. Identifying and avoiding these areas of potential entrapment is using our God-given sound mind as a first line of defense against the enemy.

Israel's second enemy was less obvious, but every bit as dangerous. It was the enemy from within. For four hundred years they had been victimized, brutally abused, and murdered by Pharaoh's guards. During those years, a healthy dose of fear was necessary for survival. Now they were free, and since fear has no place in God's kingdom, they were forced to learn new patterns of behavior. In a spiritual sense we are much like the Israelites. Prior to entering into Covenant with God, we developed unproductive patterns of behavior. Whatever it took to be noticed, to have our needs met, or to control others, we did. Since such behavior has no place in God's kingdom, we must learn new responses. The first step toward that end is to use our God-given sound mind to acknowledge the reality of these behavior patterns in our lives, patterns that have become so entrenched in us that when a situation arises, our flesh wants to respond by falling into that same old groove. Taking note of the situations which elicit these old, destructive responses, we identify our enemy from within.

After utilizing our sound mind and taking every common-sense step to protect ourselves and the enemy still shows up, what are we to do? Keeping in mind that these stories have been recorded for our example, let's consider what Moses did. Moses said to the frightened Israelites, "*The Lord will fight for you.*" When we have done all that we can to avoid entrapment, and find ourselves face to face with the enemy, God makes a way of escape for us, as surely as He parted the Red Sea and destroyed the enemy of Israel.

Remember, the Israelites had to move. Had they remained where they were, they would have been recaptured. God always provides a way of escape, but it is our responsibility to take it. First Corinthians 10:13 says, "*No temptation* has overtaken you but such as is common to man; and God is faithful, who will not allow you to be tempted beyond what you are able, but with the temptation will provide the way of escape also, that you may be able to endure it."* As God's Covenant partners, we are no longer in bondage to the enemy from within or without. In every situation, we have a split second to decide whether to put on the robe of our Covenant Partner, or rely upon our own strength. The decision rests with us.

THE CUTTING OF COVENANT

During their 430-year-stay in the land of Egypt, the Israelites grew considerably from Jacob's original entourage. As they exited Egypt, the twelve tribes of Israel numbered six hundred thousand men, plus women and children. You would think that their miraculous deliverance would have made them happy, but that was not the case. Too soon they forgot, and Moses had his hands full with these grumbling, complaining people. God came to his assistance by giving laws which set perimeters. He told Moses to call the people together and tell them, *"If you will indeed obey My voice and keep My covenant, then you shall be My own possession among all the peoples, for all the earth is Mine"* (Exodus 19:5). Moses did as God commanded, and the people replied, *Náaseh 'Nishmah* which means "we agree to do even before we have listened." That being the case, God directed Moses to a mountain top, where He dictated the laws which were to govern His people. We call these the Ten Commandments.

However, in addition to the first ten, there were laws which addressed personal injuries, sanitation, property rights, and national feast days. Other sundry laws dealt with money, morality, the land, the tabernacle, and the Sabbath. As their God, He was involved in every area of their lives. Moses recounted all that God had spoken to him, and once again the people exclaimed, *"All the words which the Lord has spoken we will do!"* (Exodus 24:3). Since they expressed their desire to be God's people, Moses carefully recorded all the words of the Lord into a book which came to be known as "The Book of the Law" or "The Book of the Covenant." Then he began to prepare for the ceremony of cutting Covenant. He built an altar with twelve pillars, representing the twelve tribes of Israel. Young men were instructed to make peace offerings, carefully reserving the animal blood. Moses placed half of the blood in basins. The other half, he sprinkled on the altar. Then he took the Book of the Law and read it to the people. *"All that the Lord has spoken we will do, and we will be obedient!"* they promised for the third time (Exodus 24:7). Moses then led the people into Covenant, by sprinkling them with the blood, and declaring *"Behold, the blood of the Covenant, which the Lord has made with you in accordance with all these words"* (Exodus 24:8). Every descendent of Jacob was now in Covenant with God. We call this "The Old Covenant" or the "Covenant of the Law." It was a continuation of the original Covenant promised to Adam and Eve, cut with Abraham, and passed on to Isaac and Jacob. It had simply broadened in scope to include all of Jacob's descendants, now known as the twelve tribes of Israel.

The Israelites Enter God's Covenant

God said to Moses, *"Let them construct a sanctuary, for Me that I may dwell among them"* (Exodus 25:8). Not only was God's presence going to dwell within this tabernacle, but the tabernacle itself would picture the fulfillment of His Covenant. For that reason, God gave specific instructions regarding the design and building of the structure and its furnishings. Let's do a brief overview of the tabernacle to see how it depicted God's Covenant. I use the word brief, because volumes have been written concerning the symbolism of the tabernacle and its furnishings. Yet, even a brief overview will enable us to catch a glimpse of the continuity and beauty of God's eternal plan—one purpose: to restore the lost relationship; one message: a coming Messiah; one Covenant: Jesus Christ, who is the same yesterday, today, and forever.

The Forgotten Covenant

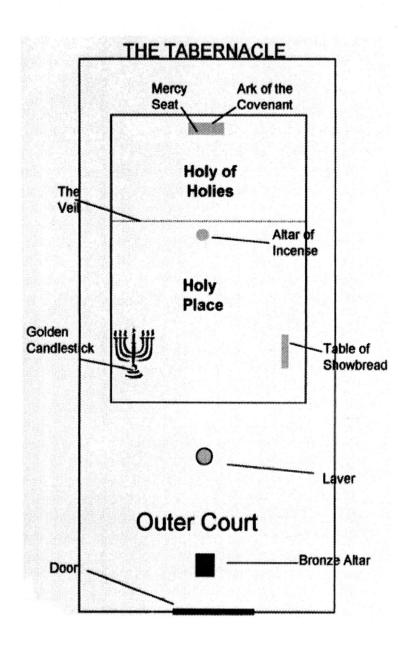

168

The Israelites Enter God's Covenant

The tabernacle was divided into three parts: the outer court, the holy place, and the Holy of Holies. The outer court was a courtyard open to all the Israelites. The Holy Place was separated from the outer court by a curtain, and only the priests were allowed to enter. Another curtain called *the veil* separated the Holy Place from the Holy of Holies, where God's presence dwelt, and only the high priest was permitted to enter, once a year on the Day of Atonement.[1]

OUTER COURT   The outer court was a yard approximately 150 feet long by 75 feet wide. It was surrounded by a high, white, linen wall which served two purposes. First, it declared "Restricted Area" to those who might ignorantly or wrongfully approach the tabernacle. Secondly, to those who were God's people, these walls became a protective barrier against the outside world. The psalms often refer to the courts of God. Psalm 100:4 bids us *"enter His gates with thanksgiving, and His courts with praise."* Capturing the emotion of those who cloistered within the white linen walls, Psalm 84:10 says, *"A day in Thy courts is better than a thousand outside. I would rather stand at the threshold of*

---

[1] Information regarding the tabernacle is taken from *The Tabernacle of Moses* by Kevin J. Conner, Bible Press, Portland, Oregon 97213.

the house of my God, than dwell in the tents of wickedness."

THE DOORWAY The only entrance into the outer court was through a colorful, curtained doorway located on the east side of the structure. It stood in stark contrast to the forbidding, white linen walls, and extended a warm welcome to those who sought entry into God's tabernacle. The blue, purple, red and white colors, designated by God, each revealed something about the coming Messiah.

> Blue speaks of the heavenly: Jesus is the Son of God.
> Purple speaks of royalty: Jesus is the King of kings.
> Red speaks of blood: Jesus is the Lamb of God who came to "*give His life as a ransom for many* (Mark 10:45).
> White indicates purity: Jesus was without sin.

The colors used in the tapestry were not all that depicted Jesus. The fact that God designed the tabernacle with only one door is highly symbolic. Jesus told His followers, "*I am the door; if anyone*

The Israelites Enter God's Covenant

enters through Me, he shall be saved, and shall go in and out, and find pasture" (John 10:9). The door to the tabernacle remained open, indicating God's willingness for all to enter into Covenant with Him. Peter told the Jews of his time, *"The Lord is not slow about His promise, as some count slowness, but is patient toward you, not wishing for any to perish but for all to come to repentance"* (2 Peter 3:9). Even the fact that the door was located on the east side is significant. When God removed Adam and Eve from the Garden of Eden, He placed an angel at the east side of the garden to guard the way to the tree of life (Genesis 3:24). When the wise men came to worship the baby Jesus, they said, *"We saw His star in the east, and have come to worship Him"* (Matthew 2:2).

THE BRONZE ALTAR

When entering the outer court, one immediately came face to face with the bronze altar (some versions of the Bible refer to it as the brass altar) It was the first and largest piece of furniture within the tabernacle, and therefore, could not be overlooked. Constructed of acacia wood, overlaid with bronze (brass), it was used for the sacrificing of animals. In the Scriptures, brass or bronze speaks of judgment. The altar placed directly in front of the entrance symbolized the fact that when approaching God, man must first deal with the issue of sin. He must first acknowledge that he is separated from God, and powerless to remedy the estrangement. The sacrificing of an unblemished male animal on this altar, foreshadowed the sacrificial death of Jesus, the Lamb of God, whose shed blood provides forgiveness to all who choose to enter into Covenant with Him.

THE LAVER   Located directly beyond the bronze altar was a copper water basin called the laver. God required that the priests wash their hands and feet before entering the Holy Place or making offerings at the bronze altar. Failure to do so would result in their death. The placement of the laver continues the symbolism as it paints a progressive picture. We enter into Covenant with God through Jesus Christ (the door), our sins are covered by the blood of the Lamb (the bronze altar), and we receive daily cleansing at the laver. Jesus said to Peter, "*If I do not wash you, you have no part with Me*" (John 13:8). Although entering into Covenant with God through Jesus Christ re-establishes our relationship with Him, we nevertheless fall short of perfection. It is the nature of the flesh to become tired, weak, hurt, crabby, and sometimes just plain rebellious, so we need daily cleansing. God says that *"if we confess our sins, He is faithful and righteous to forgive us our sins and to cleanse us from all unrighteousness"* (1 John 1:9). Ephesians 5:26 says that we are "cleansed *by the washing of water with the word"* meaning that as we daily read and appropriate God's Word in our lives, there is a continuous, deep cleansing occurring within us, which washes away old, destructive behavior patterns and replaces them with the attributes of our Covenant Partner.

THE HOLY PLACE

Positioned directly beyond the laver was the curtained doorway to the Holy Place. It was made of the same purple, blue, red, and white twisted linen that we saw in the outer court, reminding us again that Jesus is the Son of God, the King of kings, our Savior, and High Priest. The curtain was suspended by five pillars made of acacia wood overlaid with gold. Since wood is used in Scripture to symbolically represent humanity, we see that the wood overlaid in gold represents both the humanity and divinity of Jesus. The five pillars representing the Torah (the first five books of the Old Testament, called the Law), find fulfillment in Jesus Christ. Acacia boards, overlaid in pure gold formed the walls of the Holy Place, beautifully depicting the New Covenant unity of God and man. Believers are flesh (wood), yet they are covered in the robe (gold) of their Covenant Partner. The same blue, purple, red, and white linen tapestry draped from the ceiling insured that wherever one looked, he saw Jesus Christ.

TABLE OF SHEWBREAD

Located to the right of the doorway on the north side of the Holy Place was the table of shewbread. It was a small table, made of acacia wood, overlaid in pure gold, foreshadowing again the humanity and divinity of Jesus, as well as the Covenant unity of God and man. A molding of pure gold, resembling a crown encircled the top, indicating the kingship of Jesus. Every week the priests placed twelve fresh loaves of bread on this table. Jesus told His followers, *"I am the bread of life. I am the living bread that came down out of heaven; if anyone eats of this bread, he shall live forever; and the bread also which I shall give for the life of the world is My flesh"* (John 6:48, 51). The bread represented Jesus. The number twelve represented the twelve tribes of Israel and find their counterpart in Jesus' twelve disciples.

THE GOLDEN LAMPSTAND

On the south side of the Holy Place, positioned opposite the table of shewbread, was a seven-branched golden lamp stand. It was the only light within the tabernacle, symbolizing Jesus Christ as the light of the world. Jesus said, *"I am the light of the world; he who follows Me shall not walk in darkness, but shall have the light of life"* (John 8:12). The priests were instructed to fill the lamp with oil every morning and evening so that the light was perpetual, signifying that the eternal light *"which enlightens every man was coming into the world."* (John 1:9) In describing heaven, the apostle John wrote, *"They *shall not have need of the light of a lamp nor the light of the sun, because the Lord God shall illumine them"* (Revelation 22:5). The lamp stand was in the form of a tree, having a central trunk with three branches coming out on either side. God designed it so that the lamps on each side were lit by the oil from the central stem, indicating that those who are joined to God through Jesus Christ receive their life and light from Him. Jesus expressed the symbolism of the seven-branched lamp stand when He told His followers, *"I am the vine, you are the branches; he who abides in Me, and I in him, he bears much fruit; for apart from Me you can do nothing* (John 15:5). The central stem and three branches on either side made a total of seven. In Scripture, the number six represents man, and the number seven indicates completion. Therefore, the numerology indicates that God's Covenant is complete and man's relationship with God is restored in Jesus Christ.

ALTAR OF INCENSE

Beyond the golden lamp stand, situated just outside the veil which separated the Holy of Holies from the Holy Place,

The Israelites Enter God's Covenant

was the altar of incense. Twice a day, morning and evening, the priests were required to add incense so that the burning was continual. It also was constructed of acacia wood overlaid with gold, symbolizing both the humanity and deity of Jesus, and the Covenant unity of God and man. A golden crown molding around the top signified the kingship of Jesus. In the Bible, incense represents prayer and intercession. Psalm 141:2 speaks of the prayer of a believer: "*May my prayer be counted as incense before Thee.*" And Hebrews 7:25 speaks of the intercessory prayer of Jesus: "*He* [Jesus] *is able to save forever those who draw near to God through Him, since He always lives to make intercession for them.*"

Even the composition of the incense, ordered by God, had Covenant implications. Crushed bitter, sweet, salty, and fragrant spices combined to form a pleasant perfume, which burned perpetually on the altar. Because of its Covenant significance, any other form of incense was considered strange and was rejected by God.

THE VEIL

God said, "*The veil shall serve for you as a partition between the holy place and the holy of holies* (Exodus 26:33). This veil was a heavy curtain made of the same purple, blue, red, and white linen used in the others. It was a visual reminder of man's separation from God. At the moment of Jesus' death, this veil miraculously tore in two from top to bottom, indicating that Jesus had become the door through which all men were now free to enter into a Covenant relationship with God. Jew and Gentile alike could now choose to walk with God. In writing to the Hebrews, Paul said, *"We have confidence to enter the holy place by the blood of Jesus, by a new and living way which He inaugurated for us through the veil, that is, His flesh"* (Hebrews 10:19–20).

THE HOLY OF HOLIES

God's presence, described as the shekinah glory, dwelt behind the veil in the Holy of Holies. Although only the high priest was permitted to enter the Holy of Holies, God's shekinah glory was visible to all of the Israelites. The word shekinah means, *the one who dwells*, and refers to God's presence dwelling among His people. In describing Jesus, John wrote, *"And the Word became flesh and dwelt among us and we beheld His glory, glory as of the only begotten from the Father, full of grace and truth"* (John 1:14). Nothing has changed! In the person of His Holy Spirit, God now dwells within those who enter into Covenant with Him. Jesus said to His followers, *"Let your light shine before men"* (Matthew 5:16). Speaking of the Holy Spirit, Paul wrote to the Corinthian believers saying, *"We have this treasure in earthen vessels, that the surpassing greatness of the power may be of God and not from ourselves"* (2 Corinthians 4:7). God continues to dwell among His people.

THE ARK OF THE COVENANT

Located within the Holy of Holies was the most famous piece of furniture, the ark of the covenant. The ark was a box made of acacia wood overlaid in gold inside and out. This overlay, producing three layers, represented the Godhead: Father (gold), Son (wood), and Holy Spirit (gold). Inside the ark was a jar of manna from the wilderness, the stone tablets containing God's commandments, and

Aaron's rod. The ark was also adorned with a crown molding to signify the kingship of Jesus. Man crowned Him with thorns, but God crowned Him with glory and honor.

THE MERCY SEAT

The lid of the ark was a separate piece of furniture called the mercy seat. It was made of pure gold with an angel positioned on either end. Once a year on the Day of Atonement, the high priest sprinkled blood on the mercy seat to atone for the sins of the nation. If the priest were to enter the Holy of Holies without the blood, he would die. In like manner, those who refuse to enter into Covenant with God by the blood of the Lamb, will by their own choice suffer eternal separation from God. Jesus said, "*I am the way, and the truth, and the life; no one comes to the Father, but through Me*" (John 14:6).

The fact that the mercy seat was the only seat within the tabernacle and no one sat upon it is significant. Hebrews 10:11–12 says, "*And every priest stands daily ministering and offering time after time the same sacrifices, which can never take away sins;*

The Israelites Enter God's Covenant

> *but He [Jesus], having offered one sacrifice for sins for all time, sat down at the right hand of God."*

Are you beginning to appreciate the fact that God is the Master of detail? Everything He did, and every commandment He gave pointed to Jesus Christ as the fulfillment of His Covenant promise. Even the arrangement of the furniture within the tabernacle reveals the extent to which God went to ensure that His message would be understood. If you follow God's instructions regarding the placement of the furniture given in Exodus 40, and draw a line to connect the pieces, you discover that the seven pieces of furniture within the tabernacle were positioned in the form of a cross. The table of shewbread, representing the Old Covenant, and the golden lampstand, representing the New Covenant, come together in Jesus Christ. Also, according to Numbers 2, God dictated the arrangement of the camp. He commanded that the twelve tribes encamp around the tabernacle in such a way as to form a human cross consisting of 603,550 men. This cross, surrounding the tabernacle, again graphically depicts the continuity of God's Covenant. The Old is encompassed and completed in the New. (See illustrations on the following pages.)

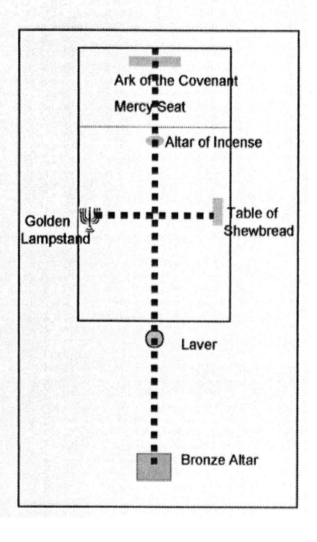

The Israelites Enter God's Covenant

The Israelites' camp as Designed by God According to Number 2

Tribes of Ephraim,
Manasseh,
Benjamin
108,100

Tribes of Rueben,
Simeon, Gad
151,450

Tabernacle

Tribes of Dan, Asher,
Naphtali
157,600

Tribes of Judah,
Issachar, Zebulun
186,400

An aerial view of the camp shows the tabernacle situated within a human cross. It is a graphic picture of the continuity of God's Covenant – the Old encompassed and completed in the New.

In looking at the tabernacle we realize that God repeated His Covenant promise over and over again. Like love notes tucked away for His beloved to find, God wrote, "I love you" in colors, in wood, in metals, in the composition of incense, in the design and placement of the furniture, and even in the arrangement of the camp. The tabernacle situated within the human cross, and God's presence dwelling within the Holy of Holies is a beautiful picture of the intimacy of the Covenant relationship. Jesus is in the Father, the Holy Spirit dwells within believers, and believers are in Jesus. Jesus said it like this: *"I am in My Father, and you in Me and I in you"* (John 14:20). At the moment of Jesus' death, as the veil miraculously tore in two from top to bottom, a door opened and all were invited into God's presence—men and women, Jews and Gentiles, slaves and free. That door remains open today, as individuals from every nation, every race, and every culture on earth continue to accept God's invitation to tabernacle with Him.

THE WILDERNESS

As the Israelites journeyed in the wilderness, an angel led them with a pillar of cloud by day and a fire by night. God fed them with manna which fell from heaven each morning, and with quail that miraculously gathered on the ground before them each evening. He satisfied their thirst with water that came forth from a rock, and for forty years, He kept their shoes and clothing from wearing out. They had every reason to praise Him and remain faithful to His Covenant, but that was not the case. And since this Cov-

The Israelites Enter God's Covenant

enant of the law was conditional, Israel's experience in the wilderness was cyclic.

Through Moses, God said to them, "*I have set before you life and death, the blessing and the curse. So choose life in order that you may live, you and your descendants, by loving the Lord your God, by obeying His voice, and by holding fast to Him*" (Deuteronomy 30:19–20). The Israelites are an excellent example of the spirit being willing, but the flesh being weak (Matthew 26:41). They wanted to be obedient, they had vowed to be obedient, but they found it to be impossible. They "*mingled with the nations, learned their practices, and served their idols* (Psalm 105:35–36). In doing so, they broke the Covenant and separated themselves from God's protection. Consequently, heathen nations defeated them in battle and took them captive. Nevertheless, God never breaks His Covenant. Therefore, when they repented and cried out to Him, He repeatedly forgave and delivered them. As part of their repentance, they sacrificed unblemished male animals to atone for their sin.

You may be wondering why innocent animals had to die, and why they had to be unblemished males. When the priests offered an animal that was blind, lame, or sick, God rejected it, called them swindlers and said, "*I am not pleased with you, nor will I accept an offering from you*" (Malachi 1:10). The reason, of course, is His Covenant. God was symbolically showing that restoration of the lost relationship would require the shed blood of His innocent, unblemished Son. Therefore, the sacrifice had to be perfect.

We should note that the people of that day had no way of understanding the symbolism. They were simply called to be obedient. Yet, because of God's love for you and me,

He made certain that this information was recorded in His Word, knowing that thousands of years later, we would be able to read the Bible and understand the typology. He made it possible for us, who have never seen Him, to find Him and grasp His eternal Covenant message of love, as we see it pictured over and over again in His Word. It is the beauty of the Scriptures. God, the Master of detail, said, "*I love those who love me; and those who diligently seek Me will find Me*" (Proverbs 8:17).

The Israelites knew that God was leading them to a land which had been promised to Abraham, but as they approached it, they became timid. "*Let us send men before us, that they may search out the land for us,*" they said (Deuteronomy 1:22). Twelve men, one from each tribe, were chosen and sent out as spies. They returned with luscious fruit as evidence of the abundance found there, but ten of the twelve gave negative reports. Being fearful, they told of giants who lived in large, fortified cities. "*We are not able to go up against the people, for they are too strong for us,*" they cried (Numbers 13:31). To the contrary, Joshua and Caleb encouraged the people, saying, "*We should by all means go up and take possession of it, for we shall surely overcome it*" (Numbers 13:30). "*If the Lord is pleased with us, then He will bring us into this land, and give it to us—a land which flows with milk and honey. Only do not rebel against the Lord; and do not fear the people of the land*" (Numbers 14:8–9). Once again the people grumbled and complained to Moses. "*Our wives and our little ones will become plunder; would it not be better to return to Egypt,*" they cried (Numbers 14:3). God was displeased. How quickly they had forgotten all He had done, and because of their grumbling and complain-

The Israelites Enter God's Covenant

ing He forbid that generation to enter the Promised Land. For forty years they wandered in the wilderness, until that entire generation died. Only then did God resume leading His people into the Promised Land with Joshua and Caleb in the forefront.

There are several things we can learn from this story. First, we see an example of God's provision for those who belong to Him. He gave the Israelites everything they needed to physically and spiritually survive in the wilderness. For forty years, He faithfully led them, fed them, protected them, and even kept their shoes and clothing from wearing out. He gave them laws which, if obeyed, insured their physical and spiritual well-being, and separated them from the heathen nations. They were His people and He took excellent care of them, but when it was time to face the giants, they forgot about Him, and became gripped with fear. God had bound Himself to them in Covenant, yet they didn't trust Him.

It is easy to criticize the Israelites, but the truth is that when we allow negativity and doubt to rob us of God's peace, we are behaving just as they did. Peter is a good example of what can happen when we focus on a problem, rather than on God. Peter was in a boat with the other disciples when they saw Jesus walking toward them on the water. Peter said, *"Lord, if it is You, command me to come to You on the water"* (Matthew 14:28). Jesus replied, "Come on," and Peter boldly climbed out of the boat. With his gaze fixed upon Jesus, oblivious to the wind and the waves billowing at his feet, he walked across the water. It must have been a marvelous sight to see, but it didn't last long. The instant Peter looked away from Jesus and considered the menacing waves, he became frightened and began to sink. Jesus grabbed him, and pulling him from the waves, He said, "*O you of little faith, why did you doubt?*" (Matthew 14:31).

We all know what it feels like to be afraid. Most believers can identify with Peter's experience. Facing a problem of giant proportions, we muster all the faith we can and boldly declare, "God, I am going to trust You no matter what happens." Yet, if the problem lasts a little longer than we anticipated, or things move in a direction we hadn't considered, we panic, focus on the problem, and begin sinking beneath the waves of despair. If we could hear God's audible voice, I believe He would ask us the same question He asked Peter, "*Why did you doubt?*" Jesus has assured us that "*all things are possible with God*" (Mark 10:27). We doubt, because we fail to understand the Covenant relationship, and Covenant is the bedrock of God's promises. If He were not a Covenant-keeping God, there would be nothing on which to base our faith. He could change His mind, and leave us to fend for ourselves. However, since He always keeps His Covenant, His promises offer eternal peace and security to His partners. God said to the prophet Hosea, "*My people are destroyed for lack of knowledge*" (Hosea 4:6). We are only able to surrender ourselves to God to the degree in which we trust Him. Since trust is based solely on God's faithfulness to His Covenant, an understanding of the Covenant relationship is imperative. Jesus said, "*You shall know the truth, and the truth shall make your free*" (John 8:32). We are set free from worry and doubt, fear and insecurity, weakness and guilt, by living in and understanding the Covenant relationship. We are free to express our love for God in any manner we choose: singing, dancing, kneeling, standing, or silently bowing our heads, because God is listening to our hearts. He literally dwells within His Covenant partners, and nothing can impose restrictions upon, nor dissolve that union.

THE PROMISED LAND

An incident which took place in the wilderness prevented Moses from entering the Promised Land. While the Israelites were camped at a place called Rephidim, they complained because there was no water. So God led Moses to a huge rock and said, *"I will stand before you there on the rock at Horeb, and you shall strike the rock, and water will come out of it, that the people may drink"* (Exodus 17:6). Moses did as God instructed and water gushed forth from the rock. Later, arriving at a place called Kadesh, they found themselves in the same situation. Once again they complained, and Moses took the problem to God. This time, God told him to speak to the rock and water would come forth. Moses was so angry and frustrated with the people that instead of speaking to the rock, he struck it twice. Water came forth, but God was angry with him. He said, *"Because you have not believed Me, to treat Me as holy in the sight of the sons of Israel, therefore you shall not bring this assembly into the land which I have given them"* (Numbers 20:12).

This seems like stiff punishment, unless we consider what happened in the light of God's Covenant. Remember, everything God did pointed to the fulfillment of His Covenant. So let's look at what the rock represented. Paul said to believers in Corinth, *"For I do not want you to be un-*

aware, brethren, that our fathers were all under the cloud, and all passed through the sea . . . and all drank the same spiritual drink, for they were drinking from a spiritual rock which followed them; and the rock was Christ (1 Corinthians 10:1–4). Since the rock represented Jesus, we can understand why God became upset with Moses. It was permissible to strike the rock one time, because it symbolized the fact that Jesus was going to beaten and crucified one time for the fulfillment of God's Covenant. It could not be symbolically struck a second time. Jesus asked His disciples, *"Who do people say that the Son of Man is? And Simon Peter answered and said, 'Thou art the Christ, the Son of the living God.' And Jesus answered and said to him, 'Blessed are you, Simon Barjona, because flesh and blood did not reveal this to you, but My Father who is in heaven. And I also say to you that you are Peter, and upon this rock I will build My church; and the gates of Hades shall not overpower it'"* (Matthew 16:13, 16–18). The rock represented Jesus Christ.

Moses never reached the Promised Land. Joshua became the Israelites' new leader, leading them triumphantly in battle, and taking possession of the land God had given them. However, after the generation of those who had taken possession of the land died, there arose a generation who did not know the Lord. They had no appreciation for the many things God had done for Israel. (Judges 2:10). Consequently, they disregarded His Covenant, intermarried with the heathen nations, and worshipped foreign gods. God sent prophets to warn them. When they repented, He forgave them. If they did not, they suffered the consequences of being separated from Him. They were defeated in battle, and were taken into captivity by heathen nations, some-

The Israelites Enter God's Covenant

times for as long as seventy years. When they had a righteous leader, they remained faithful to their God. When there was no one to lead them, they slipped back into old, destructive patterns of behavior. Their history is sadly cyclic. Times when they obeyed God's Covenant and prospered were followed by times of compromise, disobedience, and defeat.

If those living only one generation removed from the miracles involved in inheriting the Promised Land forgot God's Covenant, something was obviously wrong. The preceding generation had failed to follow God's instructions. He said to them, *"These words, which I am commanding you today, shall be on your heart; and you shall teach them diligently to your sons, and shall talk of them when you sit in your house, and when you walk by the way, and when you lie down, and when you rise up"* (Deuteronomy 6:6–7). Had they done these things, their children would have known God's Covenant. This is a clear indication of the responsibility of parents to teach their children. If children are taught God's Word, see it practically applied to everyday situations, and witness the faithfulness of God in matters concerning their own families, it becomes easier for them to find God. Sometimes when speaking to our children, it seems as if our words fall on deaf ears, but God assures us that His word never returns to Him void. He said, *"So shall My word be which goes forth from My mouth; it shall not return to Me empty, without accomplishing what I desire, and without succeeding in the matter for which I sent it"* (Isaiah 55:11). And Proverbs 22:6 promises that if we *"train up a child in the way he should go, even when he is old, he will not depart from it."*

The Forgotten Covenant

If only one generation removed from the wilderness experience, God's Covenant was forgotten, is it any wonder then that we struggle to understand it today? Israel ignorantly worshipped idols. We, being too sophisticated to worship a carved image, ignorantly worship religion itself. Having forgotten the basic definition of a covenant, we mistakenly assume that being a Christian means that we acknowledge Jesus' death on the cross, and live according to our understanding of Christian principles. During the Easter season, a church marquee read: 3 nails, plus 1 cross, equals 4 given. The message, although well intended, perpetuates the misconception. Jesus gave His life in order to *offer* forgiveness. He cut God's Covenant making it available to all mankind, but His death does not extend forgiveness carte blanche. It is not a blanket, automatically covering the whole of humanity. Jesus' death was the fulfillment of God's Covenant, and a covenant by its definition requires the personal commitment and faithfulness of the parties involved. As the Israelites entered into the Covenant, they received the blood sprinkled upon them, and were required to make a Covenant commitment. Today, in like manner, the blood of Jesus is applied to individual hearts, one person at a time. Paul emphasized the fact that Christianity is a Covenant relationship when he wrote to the Hebrews saying, "*Jesus is the mediator of a new covenant. He is also the mediator of a better covenant, which has been enacted on better promises*" (Hebrews 12:24, 8:6). Only as the blood of Jesus Christ is applied to an individual's heart as he enters into Covenant with God does "3 nails, plus 1 cross, equal 4 given." Covenant was God's idea. It is His love, His sacri-

The Israelites Enter God's Covenant

fice, and His invitation, requiring a personal response from each of us.

Israel took a giant step in the wrong direction by insisting upon having an earthly king like the heathen nations. Granting their request, God anointed Saul to be Israel's first king, and the people loved him. He was a big, handsome, valiant warrior, who epitomized their idea of royalty. *"Now we have someone who will lead us spiritually and be feared among the heathen nations,"* they thought. But Saul fell short. His arrogance led him to disobey God on more than one occasion; and as you will recall, God removed the kingdom from him and gave it to David.

Chapter 12

HONORING THE COVENANT

(King David)

My lovingkindness I will keep for him [David] forever, and My Covenant shall be confirmed to him. So I will establish his descendants forever, and his throne as the days of heaven (Psalm 89:28–29).

God made extraordinary promises to David, the next link in His Covenant chain. Regarding David's throne, God said, *"Your throne shall be established forever"* (2 Samuel 7:16). Speaking of his descendants, God promised, *"I will establish his descendants forever, and his throne as the days of heaven"* (Psalms 89:29). Praising David's character, God declared, *"He is a man after My heart, who will do all My will"* (Acts 13:22). David was a man after God's own heart, and his throne and descendants are eternal. Let's look at these individually.

What did God mean when He said that David's throne would be established forever? Israel has no king today. The last of David's bloodline to occupy the throne was Jehoiachin, and that was hundreds of years before the time of Jesus. Obviously, God's promise had Covenant implications, and when viewed in that light we understand that David's throne has been established forever because Jesus was of the lineage of King David. (You can see this on the genealogy chart.) In writing to the Hebrews, Paul said, *"He [Jesus], having offered one sacrifice for sins for all time, sat down at the right hand of God, waiting from that time onward until His enemies be made a footstool for His feet"* (Hebrews 10:12–13). Jesus now sits on an eternal throne.

Who are these eternal descendants of David? It may surprise you to learn that ALL who enter into God's Covenant, Jew and Gentile alike, become spiritual descendants of King David. Addressing a group of self-righteous Jews who thought themselves superior because of their Jewish heritage, the apostle Paul said, *"For he is not a Jew who is one outwardly; neither is circumcision that which is outward in the flesh. But he is a Jew who is one inwardly; and circumcision is that which is of the heart, by the Spirit, not by the letter; and his praise is not from men, but from God* (Romans 2:28–29). Note the core of God's Covenant in Paul's words. Christianity goes beyond external laws and ceremonies. It is an internal love relationship of the heart.

God promised that the Messiah would come from Abraham's lineage and that his descendants would be given a land of their own, but a relationship with God was never exclusively reserved for Abraham's descendants. From the beginning, God's desire was that ALL men, Jew and Gentile alike, would enter into Covenant with Him. David has an everlasting throne and his descendants live eternally because Jesus Christ, the King of kings and the Lord of lords, sits upon that eternal throne, bidding individuals from every tribe, race, and nation to enter into Covenant with Him.

David was far from perfect, so why is he described as a man after God's own heart? Perhaps one reason is that in spite of his shortcomings, David was faithful! He never worshipped other gods. His infinite love for God found expression in worship which was theretofore never known in Israel. For instance, when David constructed his tabernacle, he omitted the Holy of Holies. The ark of the covenant was placed in the center of the tabernacle, in the midst of the people, where it was surrounded by musicians and worshippers, who sang, danced, and praised God twenty-four hours a day. It was a beautiful picture of God dwelling among His people, and no one was more aware of His presence than David. Without reservation, David openly shared his heart and his life with his Covenant Partner.

Years after David's death, when Israel forsook God's Covenant and the tabernacle of David had become a mere memory, God spoke through the prophet Amos, saying, *"I will rebuild the tabernacle of David which has fallen, and I will rebuild its ruins, and I will restore it, in order that the rest of mankind may seek the Lord, and all the Gentiles who are called by My name"* (Acts 15:16–17). God revealed His heart in these words, indicating again that His desire has always been for men to walk in Covenant with Him. Second Peter 3:9 reaffirms this, saying that God *"is not wishing for any to perish but for all to come to repentance."* The tabernacle of David has been restored in Jesus Christ, and God once again dwells among His people. The indwelling of His Holy Spirit within believers makes this Covenant union the epitome of intimacy, unmatched by any human bond. Calling them His beloved, God joyously walks with those who bear His name—loving, leading, strengthening, healing, protecting, and ultimately taking them home to be with Him forever.

David's uninhibited expression of praise revealed just a part of his heart. We get a better idea by observing his behavior in a few of his darker moments. Second Samuel 24 tells about a time when David deliberately disobeyed God by taking a census of his army. Afterwards, being troubled in his heart, he said to the Lord, *"I have sinned greatly in what I have done. But now, O Lord, please take away the iniquity of Thy servant, for I have acted very foolishly"* (2 Samuel 24:10). In response, God gave David a choice. He told him to choose one of the following as a consequence of his disobedience: seven years of famine to come upon the land, three months of defeat by his enemies, or three days of pestilence by the hand of God. David chose the three days of pestilence, saying, *"I am in great distress. Let us now fall into the hand of the Lord for His mercies are great, but do not let me fall into the hand of man"* (2 Samuel 24:14). When the pestilence came and David saw that his people were dying, he cried out to the Lord saying, *"It is I who have sinned, and it is I who have done wrong; but these sheep, what have they done? Please let Thy hand be against me and against my father's house"* (2 Samuel 24:17). Do you see David's heart? He made no excuses for his behavior, but rather confessed and ran into the arms of his Covenant Partner. When he saw his people suffering the consequences of his sin, he begged that they be spared. David was humble, merciful, and faithful, truly, a man after God's own heart. Now let's contrast this by looking at King Saul in a similar situation.

During a time of battle, God instructed Saul to utterly destroy all of the Amalekites and all of their possessions. *"But Saul and the people spared Agag (the King) and the best of the sheep, the oxen, the fatlings, the lambs, and all that was good, and were not willing to destroy them utterly; but everything despised and worthless, that they utterly destroyed"* (1 Samuel 15:9). After the battle, Saul set up a monument for himself, proudly announcing to the prophet Samuel, *"I have carried out the command of the Lord"* (1 Samuel 15:12–13). With a questioning frown, Samuel replied, "Oh, really?" *"Then what is this bleating of the sheep in my ears, and the lowing of the oxen which I hear?* (1 Samuel 15:14). *"Why did you not obey the voice of the Lord, but rushed upon the spoil and did what was evil in the sight of the Lord?"* Saul's countenance must have grown stern, as he became defensive. *"I did obey the voice of the Lord,"* he argued. *"But the people took some of the spoil, sheep and oxen, the choicest of the things devoted to destruction, to sacrifice to the Lord your God at Gilgal"* (1 Samuel 15:19–21). Do you see Saul's heart? He was not the least bit repentant. He deliberately disobeyed God, then proudly set up a monument to himself, as if he had won the battle without God's assistance. When confronted by Samuel, Saul blamed his people. He also had the audacity to suggest that the animals were spared in order to become sacrifices to Samuel's God. The fact that Saul made reference to "Samuel's God," rather than "Saul's God," is certainly telling. Saul had no relationship with God. He was prideful, unrepentant, and had little concern for the well-being of his people. Let's look at David again in what was probably the worst mistake of his life.

One spring day, David sent his army out to battle, while he remained in Jerusalem. As he strolled upon his palace roof, he noticed a woman bathing on a nearby rooftop. Instead of turning away from the temptation, David continued to watch, and upon inquiry, learned that she was the wife of Uriah, one of his soldiers. David had a close relationship with God, and could have called upon the strength of his Covenant Partner to resist this temptation, but he didn't. He continued watching Bathsheba bathe, until a burning desire compelled him to have her brought to the palace. As a result of their affair, Bathsheba became pregnant. David, wanting to conceal the affair, ordered that Uriah be placed in the front line of the fiercest battle, and left unprotected. This, of course, resulted in Uriah's death. Afterwards, David took Bathsheba as his wife, and God sent the prophet Nathan to confront him. When Nathan spoke, David immediately confessed, *"I have sinned against the Lord"* (2 Samuel 12:13). Since he was sincerely repentant, Nathan informed him that the Lord had forgiven him, but that the child would die, because David's actions were blasphemous. At the appointed time, Bathsheba gave birth to a son, and God caused the child to become ill. David fasted and prayed for seven days, grieving over God's judgment. When the child died on the seventh day, he arose, washed himself, and returned to the house of the Lord to worship.

Once again we catch a glimpse of the heart of this man, David. We can only imagine how David must have been feeling, loathing what he had done, asking himself over and over again how he, the anointed of God, could have committed such heinous acts. Yielding to the lust of his flesh left David a broken man. In humility he admitted his guilt and repented of it, but the faithfulness of his heart toward God was most vividly revealed when the child died. David was saddened at the loss of the child, but not angered. Accepting God's judgment, he quickly returned to join the tabernacle singers and dancers in praise and worship. On the other hand, Saul had quite the opposite response to a judgment God issued against him, as seen in the following account.

Saul and his army were poised to fight against the Philistines. God told him to wait seven days for the prophet Samuel to come and offer a burnt offering before engaging in battle. As they waited, it became apparent that Israel was outnumbered, and many of Saul's army became frightened and ran away. Saul, being concerned over these deserters, was anxious to begin the battle, and took it upon himself to assume the role of priest and offer the burnt offering. *"And it came about as soon as he finished offering the burnt offering that behold, Samuel came; and Saul went out to meet him and to greet him"* (1 Samuel 13:10). When Samuel asked why Saul had taken it upon himself to act as priest, Saul said, *"I saw that the people were scattering from me, and that you did not come within the appointed days, and the Philistines were assembling at Michmash . . . So I forced myself and offered the burnt offering"* (1 Samuel 13:11–12). Then, speaking through Samuel, God said to Saul, *"You have acted foolishly, you have not kept the commandment of the Lord your God, which He commanded you, for now the Lord would have established your kingdom over Israel forever. But now your kingdom shall not endure. The Lord has sought out for himself a man after His own heart, and the Lord has appointed him as ruler over His people, because you have not kept what the Lord commanded you"* (1 Samuel 13:13–14). In chapter two of this book, regarding Jonathan and David, we saw Saul's reaction to God's judgment against him. He refused to accept it. Mentally tortured and driven by rage, Saul spent the remainder of his days resisting God's will by trying to kill David.

In looking at these events, we see the humility of David's heart contrasted by the arrogance of Saul. Both men broke God's Covenant, but Saul offered excuses for his behavior, never repented, and refused to accept God's judgment. David, being guilty of adultery and murder, seemingly far greater offenses, repented and ran into the forgiving arms of his Covenant Partner. Clearly, the difference between David and Saul was their hearts, and we have come to understand that God is always looking at the heart. David was far from perfect; yet, God never demands perfection from His Covenant partners. He requires faithfulness, and David was the embodiment of faithfulness, loving God with all his heart. When he sinned, he knew it. Grieving over the fact that he had displeased God, he readily confessed and sought God's forgiveness. His life demonstrates the fact that in our darkest hour, no matter what we have done, we can find acceptance and forgiveness in the arms of our Covenant Partner. God's forgiveness toward David was poignantly demonstrated, when Bathsheba gave birth to a second son, whom they named Solomon, and *"the Lord loved him"* (2 Samuel 12:24).

It is noteworthy that David never again failed in the area of immorality. Having experienced the weakness of his own flesh, he was a changed man. He had come to understand the necessity of relying upon the strength of his Covenant Partner. Somewhere along life's journey, you and I will also discover the weakness and depravity of our own flesh. When it happens, although it is an eye-opening, humbling experience, if we learn something about ourselves and our need for God's strength, then we too are changed and benefit from the wretched experience. Like David, we can get up and resume our walk with God, being more appreciative of His love and faithfulness toward us.

David's son, Solomon, reigned over the twelve tribes of Israel for forty years, and although he loved God, his heart was not wholly devoted to the Lord as the heart of David had been. Solomon also loved foreign women. He knew that God had commanded that they *"make no covenant with them* [heathen nations] *or with their gods"* (Exodus 23:32) yet he disobeyed. He had seven hundred wives, princesses, and concubines, which turned his heart to foreign gods. Trying to appease these women, he erected altars to their strange gods, and God's anger burned against him. God said, *"Because you have done this, and you have not kept My covenant and My statutes, which I have commanded you, I will surely tear the kingdom from you, and will give it to your servant. Nevertheless, I will not do it in your days for the sake of your father David, but I will tear it out of the hand of your son"* (1 Kings 11:11–12).

God required that the Israelites remain segregated from the heathen nations to protect them. He said, *"They shall not live in your land, lest they make you sin against Me; for if you serve their gods, it will surely be a snare to you"* (Exodus 23:33). Solomon's worship of foreign gods became a snare which destroyed the unity of the twelve tribes. In 2 Corinthians 6:14 Paul reiterates this same warning to those who are in Covenant with God today, saying, *"Be ye not unequally yoked together with unbelievers; for what fellowship hath righteousness with unrighteousness? And what communion hath light with darkness?"* (KJV). For our protection, believers are cautioned against yoking themselves together with unbelievers. This warning refers to a covenant relationship, as in a marriage. This is not to imply that Christians are to distance themselves from unbelievers. God's plan is that Christians interact with unbelievers, giving them an opportunity to see His Covenant in light of the everyday world.

Following the death of Solomon, during the reign of his son, Rehoboam, the kingdom of Israel divided. Ten tribes moved to the north under the reign of Jeroboam, and became known as the Northern Kingdom of Israel. The tribes of Judah and Benjamin remained in Jerusalem with Rehoboam, and were called the Southern Kingdom of Judah.

From the day that Israel divided, the Northern Kingdom was in spiritual trouble. King Jeroboam forbid his people to worship in Jerusalem, forcing them instead to worship golden idols in the land of Samaria. One day while Jeroboam was standing before one of these pagan altars, God spoke through a prophet saying, *"O altar, altar, thus says the Lord, 'Behold, a son shall be born to the house of David. Josiah by name and on you he shall sacrifice the priests of the high places who burn incense on you, and human bones shall be burned on you'"* (1 Kings 13:2). Jeroboam did not heed God's warning, and his successors became progressively more evil, reaching new heights of depravity in a king by the name of Ahab. God said that Ahab *"did more to provoke the Lord God of Israel than all the kings who were before him"* (1 Kings

16:33). Although God repeatedly sent warnings through His prophets, Israel paid no attention.

They were His chosen people, the descendants of Abraham, Isaac, and Jacob who God had faithfully led to the Promised Land, yet they chose to ignore the Covenant and to walk away from Him. After repeated warnings went unheeded, God allowed them to be taken into captivity by the Assyrians, and the Northern Kingdom ceased to exist.

The Southern Kingdom of Judah was not much better. In fact, God called Judah *"treacherous"* (Jeremiah 3:7–10) because witnessing the destruction of the Northern Kingdom had no effect upon them. The people followed in the footsteps of the Northern Kingdom, polluting the land with male prostitutes, and altars to foreign gods. Rehoboam was succeeded by eleven wicked kings and eight righteous ones, but none of the righteous kings were able to rid the land entirely of the altars. None, that is, until God's prophecy concerning a king by the name of Josiah came to pass. Approximately one hundred years after the Northern Kingdom was taken into captivity, Josiah was crowned the King of Judah, and things began to change.

Chapter 13

COVENANT IS RELATIONSHIP

King Josiah

Before him there was no king like him who turned to the LORD will all his heart and with all his soul and with all his might, according to all the law of Moses; nor did any like him arise after him (2 Kings 23:25).

Josiah was only eight years old when he was crowned King of Judah, and at the age of sixteen, he began seeking *"the God of His father David"* (2 Chronicles 34:3). God's prophecy concerning him found fulfillment when as a young man of twenty, he purged Jerusalem and Samaria (which had been the Northern Kingdom of Israel) of the altars, slaughtered the pagan priests, and burned their bones.

Prior to Josiah's reign, Judah had become steeped in idolatry. Wickedness ran rampant as God's law was ignored. Describing Judah's wretched condition, the prophet Habakkuk cried out to God saying, *"Destruction and vio-*

lence are before me; strife exists and contention arises. Therefore, the law is ignored and justice is never upheld. For the wicked surround the righteous; therefore, justice comes out perverted" (Habakkuk 1:3–4). As a by-product of Judah's condition, Solomon's temple fell into disrepair. Therefore, in the eighteenth year of Josiah's reign, when he was just twenty-six years old, he ordered the restoration of the temple. In the process of refurbishing, one of the priests discovered the book of the covenant which God have given to Moses. When Josiah heard the words of God's law, *"he tore his clothes"* lamenting, *"Great is the wrath of the Lord which is poured out on us because our fathers have not observed the word of the Lord, to do according to all that is written in this book"* (2 Chronicles 34:19–21).

Immediately, he sent messengers to inquire of a prophetess regarding these words of God. As the king, Josiah accepted full responsibility for the sins of Judah. He was young and could have blamed his wicked ancestors for his ignorance, but he didn't. He sincerely wanted to know and to please God.

The prophetess informed Josiah that God's wrath would be poured out upon Judah. However, since Josiah's heart was tender and he humbled himself when he heard the words of the law, he would be spared. God said to Josiah, *"I will gather you to your fathers and you shall be gathered to your grave in peace, so your eyes will not see all the evil which I will bring on this place and on its inhabitants"* (2 Chronicles 34:–28). Josiah was not content to merely escape God's wrath, he wanted his people to repent and to again walk in Covenant with God. Therefore, he called *"all the people, from the greatest to the least; and he read in their hearing all the words of the book of the covenant which was found in the house of the Lord"* (2 Chronicles 34:30). In their presence Josiah cut a covenant, vowing to *"walk after the Lord, and to keep His commandments and His testimonies and His statutes with all his heart and with all his soul, to perform the words of the covenant written in this book"* (2 Chronicles 34:31). Being king gave him the power to command that his people honor God's Covenant. He reinstated the Passover, and during his reign, the people *"did not turn from following the Lord God of their fathers"* (2 Chronicles 34:33).

After Josiah died in battle at the age of thirty-nine, his people returned to worshipping idols. God sent prophets to warn them, telling them that unless they repented, the nation of Babylon would defeat them, and take them into captivity for seventy years. They refused to listen to God's prophets, choosing instead to believe false prophets who insisted that God would never allow Jerusalem and His temple to be destroyed. Speaking through Jeremiah, God addressed this lie, saying, *"Do not trust in deceptive words, saying, 'This is the temple of the Lord, the temple of the Lord, the temple of the Lord.' Behold, you are trusting in deceptive words to no avail. Will you steal, murder, and commit adultery, and swear falsely and offer sacrifices to Baal, and walk after other gods that you have not known, then come and stand before Me in this house, which is called by My name, and say, 'We are delivered!' that you may do all these abominations?"* (Jeremiah 7:4, 8–10). *"Circumcise yourselves to the Lord and remove the foreskins of your heart"* (Jeremiah 4:4). Although God had compassion upon them and continued to send warnings through His prophets, *"They continually mocked the messengers of God, despised His words and scoffed at His prophets, until the wrath of the Lord arose against His people, until there was no remedy"* (2 Chronicles 36:16). Then Babylon invaded Jerusalem.

There is no better example of religion versus relationship than this story of Josiah and his people. Josiah had the heart relationship. He was intent on knowing God and walking with Him in the intimacy of His Covenant. On the other hand, the people were simply coerced into external acts of obedience. They offered the required sacrifices and observed the commanded feast days, but their hearts remained far from God. *"Judah did not return to Me with all her heart, but rather in deception,"* God declared (Jeremiah 3:10). Do you see that Christianity is not a religion, but rather an intimate, covenant relationship of the heart?

Over a span of nineteen years, Babylon invaded Jerusalem three times, taking ten thousand captives, including the royal family, officials, Israel's mighty men of valor, and all the craftsmen and smiths. Only the poorest were left behind. Yet amid the calamity, God's hand of mercy can be seen. In order to minister to His people who were displaced in Babylon for seventy years, God allowed the prophet Ezekiel to be taken captive, while Jeremiah remained behind to minister to those who were left in Jerusalem. At one point, God instructed Jeremiah to write a letter of encouragement to those who were in captivity. This is what he wrote:

> *Thus says the LORD of hosts, the God of Israel, to all the exiles whom I have sent into exile from Jerusalem to Babylon.* "*Build houses and live in them; and plant gardens, and eat their produce. Take wives and become the*

fathers of sons and daughters, and take wives for your sons and give your daughters to husbands, that they may bear sons and daughters; and multiply there and do not decrease. And seek the welfare of the city where I have sent you into exile, and pray to the Lord on its behalf; for in its welfare you will have welfare." (Jeremiah 29:4–7)

When seventy years have been completed for Babylon, I will visit you and fulfill My good word to you, to bring you back to this place. (Jeremiah 29:10)

During the days of Judah's captivity, Babylon came under the rule of Persia. And at the completion of seventy years, *"The Lord stirred up the spirit of Cyrus king of Persia"* so that he issued the following decree:

The Lord, the God of heaven, has given me all the kingdoms of the earth, and He has appointed me to build Him a house in Jerusalem, which is in Judah. Whoever there is among you of all His people, may His God be with him! Let him go up to Jerusalem which is in Judah, and rebuild the house of the Lord, the God of Israel; He is the God who is in Jerusalem. (Ezra 1:1–3)

What a proclamation! Cyrus was a heathen king, and yet he was releasing God's people and commissioning them to rebuild the temple in Jerusalem. He also returned all of the temple articles which had been taken by Nebuchadnezzar.

It took over forty years for them to clean up the debris, and complete the rebuilding of the temple and Jerusalem. When the work was finally completed and the city once again inhabited by God's people, they rejoiced, exclaiming to God, *"Thou hast fulfilled Thy promise, for Thou art righteous"* (Nehemiah 9:8). Once again sacrifices burned upon the bronze altar and the holy feasts were observed, but one thing was noticeably missing—the ark of the covenant. Some believe that Jeremiah hid the ark at the time of the invasions to keep it from falling into heathen hands, and it was never recovered. Some assume that it was taken by Nebuchadnezzar's army, although it was not listed among the articles carried to Babylon. Others spiritualize its disappearance, suggesting that God supernaturally removed the ark. At this point, the missing ark remains a mystery. Perhaps God arranged for the ark's disappearance in order to prepare Judah for the coming Messiah. When Jesus walked among men, He proclaimed, *"He who has seen Me has seen the Father."* After His death and resurrection, the Holy Spirit came to indwell believers, making the ark obsolete.

Although this remnant of God's people began with the best of intentions, in time they slipped back into old patterns of behavior. Their priests defiled God's altar by sacrificing sick and lame animals. They were sloppy in their devotion to God's law, giving incorrect instructions to the people. They showed partiality, allowed intermarriage with foreigners, and permitted divorce. It comes as no surprise that the people followed suit, becoming greedy and arrogant. Robbing God of His tithes and offerings, they defiantly declared, *"It is vain to serve God; and what profit is it that we have kept His charge, and that we have walked in mourning before the Lord of hosts? So now we call the arrogant blessed; not only are the doers of wickedness built up, but they also test God and escape"* (Malachi 3:14–15). After pointing out their transgressions and warning them, God gave one last prophecy regarding the fulfillment of His covenant. He said to them, *"Behold, I am going to send My messenger, and he will clear the way before Me. And the Lord, whom you seek, will suddenly come to His temple; and the messenger of light, behold, He is coming"* (Malachi 3:1). Judah had God's written laws, they heard His voice through the prophets, and now they had His promise that the fulfillment of the Covenant was imminent. There was nothing more to be said so God became silent.

Chapter 14

GOD'S COVENANT FULFILLED

(Jesus)

After four hundred years of silence, God sent the angel Gabriel to deliver private, covenant-related messages to two individuals. The first was delivered to a priest by the name of Zacharias. Since he and his barren wife, Elizabeth, were advanced in years, Zacharias was shocked to hear Gabriel declare, *"Your wife Elizabeth will bear you a son, and you will give him the name John. And it will be he who will go as a forerunner before Him (Jesus) in the spirit and power of Elijah"* (Luke 1:13, 17). Zacharias had difficulty believing the message, therefore Gabriel caused him to become mute, saying, *"You shall be silent and unable to speak until the day when these things take place, because you did not believe my words, which shall be fulfilled in their proper time"* (Luke 1:20).

Six months later, God sent Gabriel to deliver His Covenant message to Elizabeth's cousin, Mary. Mary was a virgin of the lineage of King David, engaged to a man named Joseph, also one of David's descendants. When Mary saw the angel, she became frightened, but Gabriel reassured her with these words. *"Do not be afraid, Mary; for you have found favor with God. And behold, you will conceive in your womb, and bear a son, and you shall name Him Jesus. He will be great, and will be called the Son of the Most High; and the Lord God will give Him the throne of His father David; and He will reign over the house of Jacob forever; and His kingdom will have no end* (Luke 1:30–32). Being a virgin, Mary questioned how all this would take place, and Gabriel explained: *"The Holy Spirit will come upon you, and the power of the Most High will overshadow you; and for that reason the holy offspring shall be called the Son of God. And behold, even your relative Elizabeth has also conceived a son in her old age; and she who was called barren is now in her sixth month. For nothing will be impossible with God."*

"Behold the bondslave of the Lord; be it done to me according to your word," Mary replied, bowing in reverence and submission (Luke 1:35–38).

Elizabeth gave birth to her son, and when Zacharias indicated that the child was to be named John as instructed by the angel, his speech returned. Filled with the Holy Spirit, he prophesied concerning the child: *"Blessed be the Lord God of Israel, for He has visited us and accomplished redemption for His people, and has raised up a horn of salvation for us in the house of David His servant, as He spoke by the mouth of His holy prophets from of old to show mercy toward our fathers, and to remember His holy covenant. And you child, will be called the prophet of the Most High; for you will go on before the Lord to prepare His ways; to give to His people the knowledge of salvation by the forgiveness of their sins; because of the tender mercy of our God* (Luke 1:68–70, 72, 76–77).

Six months after the birth of John, the baby Jesus was born in a manger in Bethlehem. Who was He? So that we don't get lost in the familiarity of these events, let's view them from the perspective of God's Covenant. The birth of Jesus and the events leading up to it clearly indicate that He was the long-awaited, promised Messiah, as He perfectly fulfilled all prophecies concerning Him. Here are just a few:

- He was of the lineage of King David (Isaiah 9:6–7).
  "For a child will be born to us, a son will be given to us; and the government will rest on His shoulders; and His name will be called Wonderful, Counselor, Mighty God, Eternal Father, Prince of Peace. There will be no end to the increase of His government or of peace, on the throne of David and over his kingdom, to establish it and to uphold it with justice and righteousness from then on and forevermore."
- He was born of a virgin (Isaiah 7:14).
  "Therefore the Lord Himself will give you a sign; Behold a virgin will be with child and bear a son, and she will call His name Immanuel."
- He was born in Bethlehem (Micah 5:2).
  "But as for you, Bethlehem Ephrathah, too little to be among the clans of Judah, from you One will go forth for Me to be ruler in Israel. His goings forth are from long ago, from the days of eternity."
- His was preceded by a prophet who called men to repentance (Malachi 3:1).

"'Behold, I am going to send My messenger, and he will clear the way before Me. And the Lord whom you seek, will suddenly come to His temple; and the messenger of the covenant, in whom you delight, behold, He is coming,' says the Lord of hosts."

"A voice is calling 'Clear the way for the LORD in the wilderness; Make smooth in the desert a highway for our God'" (Isaiah 40:3).

In addition to the fulfilled prophecies, supernatural events surrounded the birth of Jesus:

- Angels appeared to shepherds on a hillside.

"And in the same region there were some shepherds staying out in the fields, and keeping watch over their flock by night. And an angel of the Lord suddenly stood before them, and the glory of the Lord shone around them, and they were terribly frightened. And the angel said to them, 'Do not be afraid; for behold, I bring you good news of a great joy which shall be for all the people; for today in the city of David there has been born for you a Savior, who is Christ the Lord.'" (Luke 2:8–11).

And suddenly there appeared with the angel a multitude of the heavenly host praising God (Luke 2:13).

- A star appeared in the east, proclaiming His birth.

"Now after Jesus was born in Bethlehem of Judea in the days of Herod the king, behold, magi from the east arrived in Jerusalem, saying, 'Where is He who has been born King of the Jews? For we saw His star in the east, and have come to worship Him'" (Matthew 2:1–2).

God's Covenant Fulfilled

It seems a bit odd that the Son of God, the long-awaited fulfillment of God's Covenant, came at a time when there was no room for Him in all of Bethlehem. Surely the God who miraculously delivered His people from Egyptian bondage, cared for them in the wilderness for forty years, and led them into the Promised Land could have arranged a suitable birthplace for His son. Or could it be that God intentionally chose the manger? If so, why would He do that? I believe the fact that there was no room for Jesus in all of Bethlehem is indicative of the fact that there is no room for Him in our lives. The needs and desires of our flesh fill every nook and cranny of our being, as we feed it, clothe it, promote it, exercise it, and pamper it. Once a week, our thoughts may turn toward God for an hour or so, but if the sermon gets a little long, our minds begin to wander and we soon find ourselves quietly slipping out the door, mumbling, "I'm sorry God. I know You'll understand." This weekly, obligatory appearance might be acceptable had Jesus come to introduce a new religion, but He didn't. Jesus Christ cut God's Covenant, and we have already seen that Covenant is a matter of the heart.

Had Jesus been the founder of a new religion, His birth would have gone unnoticed with notoriety coming later, when He matured and introduced His new spiritual persuasion. After all, there was nothing extraordinary about the birthing process. Jesus came into this world in the usual manner. Nevertheless, when He arrived, that manager in Bethlehem could not contain the glorious presence of the Son of God—The King of kings—The Lord of lords—the divine fulfillment of God's Covenant promise. The radiance of His being seeped beyond the walls of that stable, summoning a choir of angels, who announced His birth to stunned shepherds on a hillside. The psalmist said that in Jesus *"lovingkindness and truth met together, and righteousness and peace kissed each other"* (Psalms 85:10). The sheer force of lovingkindness, truth, righteousness, and peace fused within God's creative power, ignited a shimmering new star in the heavens which illuminated the entire universe, and signaled Jesus' arrival to three wise men some distance away. There was no room for Jesus in the inn, yet when He came, His presence permeated our universe. This mirrors what occurs in the lives of individuals today as they enter into Covenant with Him. Our common sense, earthly mentality tells us that we have no room for God in our lives. Yet, as we surrender ourselves to Him, at the fusion of our obedience and His faithfulness, there is a supernatural explosion of power which fills us with His presence, and radiates the light of His countenance to all around us. Jesus said, *"I am the light of the world; he who follows Me shall not walk in the darkness, but shall have the light of life"* (John 8:12). Instructing His disciples, Jesus said, *"Let your light shine before men in such a way that they may see your good works, and glorify your Father who is in heaven"* (Matthew 5:16). As sure as that star brightened Bethlehem's night sky, the presence of God's Holy Spirit shines forth in the lives of those who are His Covenant partners today.

Jesus was Mary and Joseph's firstborn son, therefore Jewish law required that He be presented to the priest for dedication to the Lord. As Mary and Joseph entered the temple, they found themselves to be participants in a divine appointment with an old, righteous gentleman named Simeon. God had promised Simeon that he would not see death until he had seen the Messiah. That day, as he held Jesus in his arms, Simeon lifted his eyes toward heaven and cried, *"Now Lord, Thou dost let Thy bond-servant depart in peace, according to Thy word; for my eyes have seen Thy salvation, which Thou hast prepared in the presence of all peoples, A light of revelation to the Gentiles, and the glory of Thy people Israel"* (Luke 2:29–32). There was no doubt in Simeon's mind that nestled peacefully against his chest lay the fulfillment of God's Covenant, the door through which all men could enter and once again walk with God.

Jesus' cousin John grew into adulthood to become the literal fulfillment of this prophecy given by Isaiah: *"A voice is calling, 'Clear the way for the Lord in the wilderness; make smooth in the desert a highway for our God'"* (Isaiah 40:3). John is considered to be the last of the Old Testament prophets. His voice boomed across Judea, preaching an uncompromised message of repentance; multitudes came to be baptized by him. He was called John the Baptist, and some wondered if he might even be the Christ. John corrected them, saying, *"I baptize you with water; but He who is mightier than I is coming, and I am not fit to untie the thong of His sandals. He Himself will baptize you in the Holy Spirit and fire"* (Luke 3:16). *"He must increase, but I must decrease"* (John 3:30).

One day as John was baptizing in the river, Jesus approached. Immediately, John stopped, and with a thunderous voice bravely introduced Jesus to a lost and waiting world with these words, *"Behold the Lamb of God who takes away the sin of the world"* (John 1:29). Knowing that Jesus was the fulfillment of God's Covenant, John protested when Jesus asked to be baptized by him. *"I have need to be baptized by*

You," John insisted. *"Permit it at this time; for in this way it is fitting for us to fulfill all righteousness"* Jesus explained (Matthew 3:14–15). As Jesus came up out of the water, the heavens were opened, the Spirit of God in the form of a dove descended upon Him, and a voice out of heaven declared, *"This is My beloved Son in whom I am well-pleased"* (Matthew 3:17).

Following His baptism, Jesus went alone into the wilderness where He fasted, prayed, and at the conclusion of forty days, was tempted by Satan. He was tempted in the three areas which we have already identified—lust of the flesh, greed, and pride. Since He had not eaten for forty days, Satan suggested that Jesus use His power to turn stones into bread. Jesus replied, *"Man shall not live on bread alone, but on every word that proceeds out of the mouth of God"* (Matthew 4:4). Then, taking Him to the top of the temple, Satan tempted Him in the area of pride, chiding, *"If you are the Son of God, throw Yourself down; for it is written, 'He will give His angels charge concerning You; and on their hands they will bear You up, lest You strike Your foot against a stone'"* (Matthew 4:6). Once again, Jesus used God's Word to silence His enemy. *"On the other hand, it is written, 'You shall not tempt the Lord your God,"* He declared (Matthew 4:7). Finally, displaying all the kingdoms of the world and their glory, Satan enticed Jesus with wealth, *"All these things will I give You, if You fall down and worship me,"* he promised (Matthew 4:9). Turning to face this enemy one last time, Jesus declared, *"Be gone, Satan! For it is written, 'You shall worship the Lord your God and serve Him only'"* (Matthew 4:10). Then the devil left and angels came to minister to Him. Upon returning from the wilderness, Jesus learned

God's Covenant Fulfilled

that John the Baptist had been imprisoned for preaching against the wickedness of Herod; this event seems to have signaled the beginning of His public ministry.

What was Jesus' ministry? It was the fulfillment of this prophecy given by Isaiah regarding the coming Messiah: *The Spirit of the Lord God is upon me because the Lord has anointed me to bring good news to the afflicted; He has sent me to bind up the brokenhearted, to proclaim liberty to captives, and freedom to prisoners; to proclaim the favorable year of the Lord* (Isaiah 61:1–2).

After reading these words in the synagogue, Jesus closed the book and lifting His eyes to look into the expectant faces before Him, declared, *"Today this scripture has been fulfilled in your hearing"* (Luke 4:21). He came preaching the gospel, the long-awaited good news. *"I am the good shepherd; the good shepherd lays down His life for the sheep,"* He told them (John 10:11). Innocent blood had to be shed in order to cut God's Covenant, and Jesus was letting them know that the blood would be His.

A professing atheist, having no understanding of God's Covenant sarcastically remarked, "I don't understand how a loving God could kill His own son." The answer: He didn't. God did not kill Jesus Christ, nor did the Romans. Jesus could have escaped the cross at any time, but He willingly sacrificed His life to cut God's eternal Covenant. When His disciples grew concerned over His arrest, Jesus said to them, *"All this has taken place that the Scriptures of the prophets may be fulfilled,"* for there was no other way (Matthew 26:56). God's children were lost, separated from Him. They were kidnapped by an enemy, and Jesus' death on the cross was the only means of rescuing them. It was God's supreme act of love, providing a way home, a way back to Himself for all who want to take it. In John 15:13 Jesus said, *"Greater love has no one than this that one lay down his life for his friends."*

He proclaimed release to all who were held in captivity. saying, *"You shall know the truth, and the truth shall make you free"* (John 8:32). To the self-righteous who boasted that they were not enslaved, He said, *"Truly, truly, I say to you, every one who commits sin is the slave of sin"* (John 8:34). *If therefore the Son shall make you free, you shall be free indeed"* (John 8:36). When Jesus came to the country of the Gadarenes, *"Two men who were demon-possessed met Him as they were coming out of the tombs; they were so exceedingly violent that no one could pass by that road. And behold, they cried out, saying 'What do we have to do with You, Son of God? Have You come here to torment us before the time?'"* (Matthew 8:28–29). It appears that the demons had no difficulty recognizing Jesus as the Son of God. They knew who He was and why He had come. Scripture records that Jesus freed these men from their demonic possession; and He continues to set individuals free today. The freedom He offers is freedom from the bondage of the enemy, as well as the lusts of our flesh. Those who join themselves to Him in Covenant are no longer victims. They walk in a new-found freedom based upon the love, strength, and wisdom of their Covenant Partner. They live the abundant life He promised.

In His mercy Jesus revealed the heart of God the Father by binding up the afflicted and healing *"every kind of disease and every kind of sickness among the people"* (Matthew 4:23). Through the prophet Isaiah, God said, *"The eyes of*

God's Covenant Fulfilled

the blind will be opened, and the ears of the deaf will be unstopped. Then the lame will leap like a deer, And the tongue of the dumb will shout for joy" (Isaiah 35:5–6). Jesus is seen fulfilling this prophecy in the following accounts:

- A certain royal official whose son was sick asked Jesus to come down and heal his son; for he was at the point of death. *"Jesus said to him, 'Go your way; your son lives'"* (John 4:47–52). *"And as He passed by, He saw a man blind from birth."* Jesus said, *"While I am in the world, I am the light of the world."* Then *"He spat on the ground, and made clay of the spittle, and applied the clay to his eyes, and said to him, 'Go, wash in the pool of Siloam' And so he went away and washed, and came back seeing"* (John 9:1, 5–7).
- Jesus visited the pool at Bethesda, a place where an angel appeared periodically to stir up the water. The first person to enter the water after it was stirred by the angel received healing. A certain man was there, who had been sick for thirty-eight years. *"When Jesus saw him lying there, and knew that he had already been a long time in that condition, He said to him, 'Do you wish to get well?' The sick man answered, 'Sir, I have no man to put me into the pool when the water is stirred up, but while I am coming, another steps down before me.' Jesus said to him, 'Arise, take up your pallet, and walk.' And immediately the man became well, and took up his pallet and began to walk"* (John 5:5–9).

- When Jesus learned that Lazarus had died, He went to the cave where he was buried and prayed saying, *"'Father, I thank Thee that Thou heardest Me. And I knew that Thou hearest Me always; but because of the people standing around I said it, that they may believe that Thou didst send Me.' And when He had said these things, He cried out with a loud voice, 'Lazarus, come forth.' He who died came forth, bound hand and foot with wrappings; and his face was wrapped around with a cloth. Jesus said to them, 'Unbind him, and let him go'"* (John 11:41–44).
- "A leper came to Him, and bowed down to Him, saying, 'Lord if You are willing, You can make me clean.' And stretching out His hand, He touched him, saying, 'I am willing; be cleansed.' And immediately his leprosy was cleansed" (Matthew 8:2–3).

Jesus went "about all the cities and the villages, teaching in their synagogues, and proclaiming the gospel of the kingdom, and healing every kind of disease and every kind of sickness" (Matthew 9:35). Regarding His many miracles, the apostle John wrote, "And there are also many other things which Jesus did, which if they were written in detail, I suppose that even the world itself would not contain the books which were written" (John 21:25).

Even with Jesus standing in their midst, not everyone desired a relationship with Him. They were willing to follow Him, but only to a point. His miracles and parables were entertaining, but when He pushed for a commitment, they walked away. Jesus said to them, "*Truly, truly, I say to you, unless you eat the flesh of the Son of Man and drink His blood, you have no life in yourselves. He who eats My flesh and drinks My blood has eternal life; and I will raise him up on the last day. For My flesh is true food, and My blood is true drink. He who eats My flesh and drinks My blood abides in Me and I in him* (John 6:53–56). *This is the bread which came down out of heaven; not as the fathers ate, and died, he who eats this bread shall live forever* (John 6:58). Those who heard Jesus' words understood what He was asking of them. They knew that to eat His flesh and drink His blood meant that they would be entering into a Covenant with Him, a sacred relationship which could never be broken. Thus many of His followers left Him that day. We are not so different. Tolerating a smattering of religion, we enjoy the pageantry of seasonal religious holidays. We pride ourselves on the fact that our name is listed on a church roster, and we willingly give to the poor. However, when it comes to surrendering control of our lives, we draw the line. We also walk away from Him. Yet, His words resound with the same truth as they did two thousand years ago: *"I am the bread of life. Unless you eat the flesh of the Son of Man and drink His blood, you have no life in yourselves.* (John 6:53)

Before going to the cross, Jesus shared a Covenant meal with those disciples who were willing to join themselves to Him in Covenant. *"While they were eating, Jesus took some bread, and after a blessing, He broke it and gave it to the disciples, and said, 'Take eat; this is My body.' And He took a cup and gave thanks, and gave it to them, saying, 'Drink from it, all of you; for this is My blood of the Covenant, which is to be shed on behalf of many for forgiveness of sins'"* (Matthew

26:26–28). First Corinthians 11:25 records Jesus telling His disciples to remember him *"as often"* as they eat the bread and drink the wine. When Jesus used the words "as often," He was stressing the fact that believers are to think of Him more often than the occasional communion service at church. I believe that He meant for us who are called by His name to be so conscious of His presence, that whenever we eat a slice of bread or take a sip of wine, we are reminded of our eternal unity with the King of kings. How different our lives would be if we were to live in such awareness. The formal celebration of Communion (the Lord's Supper) in church today cannot make anyone a Christian, but those who are born-again believers find this Covenant meal transformed from a religious ritual into a tender moment of reflection, a precious reminder of their oneness with Him.

Jesus walked among men, demonstrating God's Covenant. His love and power were there for all to see, as He healed the sick, delivered the demon possessed, and raised the dead. He showed Himself to be their protector when He prevented Mary from being stoned, Peter from drowning, and the disciples from being shipwrecked. He lived before them as the personification of Covenant unity, declaring, *"The Son can do nothing of Himself, unless it is something He sees the Father doing; for whatever the Father does, these things the Son also does in like manner"* (John 5:19). On more than one occasion, He said to His followers, *"He who has seen Me has seen the Father"* for *"I and the Father are one"* (John 14:9, 10:30).

He came proclaiming the *"favorable year of the Lord"* just as Isaiah had prophesied. In the original Hebrew, that word *favorable* means a time which God Himself has chosen. This was the time, chosen by God to fulfill His Covenant. No external, religious ceremonies devised by man could restore the lost relationship. Nothing short of God's Covenant could give men a chance to once again know and walk with Him. Jesus said, *"I am the door; if anyone enters through Me, he shall be saved, and shall go in and out, and find pasture* (John 10:9). *For God so loved the world that He gave His only begotten Son, that whoever believes in Him should not perish, but have eternal life"* (John 3:16). Notice that Jesus said "whoever believes *in* Him" will be saved. Believing in Him is quite different from believing things *about* Him. All of Jesus' followers believed something about Him. Some believed Him to be a teacher, some a prophet, some a healer, and some believed Him to be insane. But only a few were willing to believe in Him.

The Greek phrase, *believe in* means to commit one's self and to entrust one's well-being to another. Christians live, move, and have their being in Jesus. There is absolutely no separation between the secular life and spiritual life of those who are in Covenant with God. By the indwelling of His Holy Spirit, God is involved in every aspect of the Christian's life. Using the word, *abide* to describe this intimacy, Jesus said to His followers, *"Abide in Me and I in you. As the branch cannot bear fruit of itself, unless it abides in the vine, so neither can you, unless you abide in Me. I am the vine, you are the branches; he who abides in Me, and I in him, he bears much fruit; for apart from Me, you can no nothing"* (John 15:4–5). Religious rituals and benevolent acts cannot restore our lost relationship with God, for He declared that *"all our righteous deeds are like a filthy garment"* (Isaiah 64:6). He does not ask us to do things *for* Him, but rather to surrender control of our lives and become joined *to* Him. Continuing on, Jesus said, *"If you keep My commandments, you will abide in My love. Just as I have kept the Father's commandments and abide in His love"* (John 15:10). *"I am in My Father, and you in Me, and I in You,"* He explained, to describe the intimate bond (John 14:20). Walking in God's Covenant means that every moment of our lives becomes a shared experience. In writing to Jews, who knew from the beginning that the promised Messiah would come from the seed of Abraham, the apostle John wrote, *"Let that abide in you which you heard from the beginning. If what you heard from the, beginning abides in you, you also will abide in the Son and in the Father"* (1 John 2:24). Offering further clarification, he went on to explain, *"The anointing which you received from Him abides in you; and you have no need for anyone to teach you; but as His anointing teaches you about all things, and is true and is not a lie, and just as it has taught you, you abide in Him"* (1 John 2:27). *"And the one who keeps His commandments abides in Him, and He in him. And we know by this that He abides in us, by the Spirit which He has given us* (1 John 3:24).

Believing and abiding in Jesus is the Covenant relationship God offers to us. There is no other way into His presence. Jesus said, "Truly, truly, I say to you, unless one is born again, he cannot see the kingdom of God" (John 3:3). As He hung on the cross in anguish, Jesus cried, "It is finished." He had finished what He had come to do. He had cut the Covenant in His own blood, giving men an opportunity to once again know and walk with God. At the moment of His death, the curtain within the tabernacle which separated the Holy of Holies from the Holy Place miraculously tore in two from top to bottom, indicating that all were now free to approach God. Referring to this act of God, Paul said, "Therefore, brethren, we have confidence to enter the holy place by the blood of Jesus, by a new and living way which He inaugurated for us through the veil, that is, His flesh" (Hebrews 10:19–20). Jesus provided the way for individuals from every culture, every race, and every generation to symbolically walk between the pieces of His flesh and enter into Covenant with God.

Throughout this book we have noted that the making of a covenant requires the shedding of blood, the exchanging of vows, and a sign which serves as a continual reminder to those involved. We have seen that Jesus fulfilled each of these requirements. Dying on the cross, He cut God's Covenant in His own blood. He vowed to never leave nor forsake those who join themselves to Him, and He sent the Holy Spirit to reside within believers as a sign of the Covenant.

The bible refers to Christians as the bride of Christ. If we remain ignorant of His Covenant, we are like a bride who vows at the altar, but never moves in with the groom. She takes his name, but she takes it in vain, because she cannot know him without abiding with him. Jesus said that believers are to *abide* in Him. It is in the abiding that we come to know Him, the powerful working of His Holy Spirit, the boundless provision of His love, and an intimacy beyond anything we can imagine. It is the abundant life He promised to all who join themselves to Him.

How do we enter into this Covenant with God?

Although it happens in an instant, and circumstances differ from person to person, the cry of a heart seeking after God remains the same—God, I want to know You. Bruce Olson, missionary to the Motilone Indians in South America, began searching for God when he was fourteen years old. The following is an excerpt from his book, *Brusco,* in which he describes his personal search for God.

> Who is my God? I asked myself again. There's the Lutheran God, whom we talk about in church. There's the God of all the Christian churches, whom we study about in school. There's the God I've been reading about in the Bible. But which of them is *my* God? It didn't seem that anybody knew the answer. The Sunday before, I had gotten enough courage to ask my Sunday school teacher. He'd smiled a big toothy smile. "Didn't you take your confirmation vows?" I knew all about confirmation. While studying for it, I had learned theology. But I wanted to know God.
>
> Surely somewhere there was someone who could help me. The apostle John had met Jesus and since then had never been the same. All the gospels told about people being changed by Jesus. I longed for a change, too. But

my God didn't care enough about me to do anything, I thought. Who is my God, anyway? Where is He? I said to myself. Maybe if I keep reading, I'll find the answer, I thought. But I didn't really expect to find something helpful. Then I came across a verse that shocked me and sent electricity jingling through my body. I sat up and read it again: "For the Son of man is come to seek and to save that which was lost." I knew God's justice, that He would judge me on the basis of my impurities—but here was a verse saying that Jesus had come to save the lost. I knew instantly whom He was talking about. Me. But how was Jesus going to save me? And from what? Was He going to do some miracle?

A verse I had read in Romans began to make sense: "If thou shalt ... believe in thine heart that God hath raised Him [Christ] from the dead, thou shalt be saved." And saved was the opposite from lost. That's all? I thought. Just believe? Shouldn't I have to do some great thing? Shouldn't I have to live a perfect life? That was the idea I had gotten from my church. 'Lord, I am frightened by You. You know I don't even like myself. Everything is messed up around me. And it's messed up in me, too. But, please, God, I want to change. I can't do it myself. And I don't understand how You can do anything within me. But Jesus, if You could change all those people in the Bible, I guess you can change me. Please Jesus, let me know You. Make me new.' And then I knew that I was being saved. I realized a peace coming into me. It wasn't something dead and passive, that peace. It wasn't just a silence ending the war inside me. It was alive, and it was making me alive. And I knew that I didn't ever want that peace, that stillness to go away. I didn't have to worry about the Lutheran God or the Christian God or anyone else's God. They weren't my problem. Jesus was my God, my personal God. And I had just talked with Him.[1]

Entering into Covenant with God is that simple. You can become a Christian today by coming just as you are, surrendering yourself completely to Him, and receiving Jesus Christ into your life. He will give you a new heart, place His Holy Spirit within you, joining Himself to you eternally. He wants you to know Him and to walk with Him. It is His eternal gift of love, and He offers it to you with no strings attached.

HOW DO YOU MAINTAIN THIS COVENANT RELATIONSHIP?

Ezekiel 36:27 tells us that the indwelling of God's Holy Spirit causes believers to keep Covenant with Him, therefore we need not be concerned about it. Before Jesus' death, the Holy Spirit was *with* believers, but He did not *indwell* them until after Jesus' resurrection. While He was on the earth, Jesus told His followers: "*I will ask the Father, and He will give you another Helper that He may be with you forever, that is the Spirit of truth, whom the world cannot receive, because it*

---

[1] *Bruchko* by Bruce Olson. Used by permission of Strang Communications Company, 600 Rinehart Road, Lake Mary, FL 32746, © 1973, 1978, 1993, 1995 by Creation House.

does not behold Him or know Him, but you know Him because He abides with you, and will be in you" (John 14:16–17). Again, making reference to the Holy Spirit, Jesus said, *"He will teach you all things, and bring to your remembrance all that I said to you"* (John 14:26). The Holy Spirit is the teacher. He enables Christians to understand and apply God's word in real-life situations. He empowers then to stand firm in the face of temptation, providing discernment, wisdom, and needed strength for every situation. Brand new baby Christians are capable of walking with God because the Holy Spirit within them is not an infant. He is the same powerful Spirit who raised Jesus from the dead, and now dwells within all those who choose to enter into Covenant with Him.

In writing to believers in Rome, Paul wrote, *"If the Spirit of Him who raised Jesus from the dead dwells in you, He who raised Christ Jesus from the dead will also give life to your mortal bodies through His Spirit who indwells you"* (Romans 8:11). The Holy Spirit is the *"friend who sticks closer than a brother"* (Proverbs 18:24). He is what makes the fulfilled New Covenant better than the Old Covenant of the law. The Israelites had God's law, and although they wanted to obey it, they could not. In their own strength, they could not defeat the lusts of their own flesh. The indwelling of God's Holy Spirit does what the Law could never do. Being intimately acquainted with us and every aspect of our lives, He is able to lead, to guide, to teach, to protect, to strengthen, and to cause us to keep Covenant with God. More intimate than a marriage relationship, God's Covenant is similar in that Christians live and share every moment of their lives with their Covenant Partner. Being one with Him, they walk in accordance with His written word, follow the voice of His Holy Spirit, and grow in their knowledge of Him, causing the love relationship to become sweeter and sweeter as the years go by.

WHAT HAPPENS IF WE BREAK THE COVENANT?

Ideally, in times of anger and stress, a believer will always pause to call upon the strength of his Covenant Partner, and therefore never make a wrong move. Since we live somewhere outside the realm of the ideal, these words from 1 John 8–10 have much to say to us: *"If we say that we have no sin, we are deceiving ourselves, and the truth is not in us. If we confess our sins, He is faithful and righteous to forgive us our sins and to cleanse us from all unrighteousness"* When we fail, we break Covenant with God. This does not mean that the Covenant is no longer valid, because God's Covenant is eternal. *He never breaks it.* However, when we take a step in the wrong direction, and allow something to come between us and our Covenant Partner, we feel miserable. It is similar to what occurs when spouses have a misunderstanding. The marriage covenant isn't dissolved because of a disagreement, but the relationship suffers, and we feel that invisible wall until apologies are made and forgiveness extended. The discomfort we experience when we displease God is a safeguard. It makes us aware that we have gotten off track, and prompts us to run to Him, confess what we've done, repent of it, and receive His forgiveness. It is what God meant when He said that He will *cause* believers to keep Covenant with Him, and undeniable proof of His indwelling presence. The Holy Spirit makes certain that those who are in Covenant with God remain faithful to Him.

God's Covenant is the ultimate love connection. It's intimate, it's powerful, and it's eternal. Not only is it eternal in the sense that it promises eternal life after death, but it gives an immediate supernatural, eternal quality of life here and now. Jesus calls it the abundant life. He said, *"I came that they might have life, and might have it abundantly"* (John 10:10). Using Moses as His spokesperson, God said to the people of the Old Covenant, *"I have set before you life and death, the blessing and the curse. So choose life in order that you may live, you and your descendants"* (Deuteronomy 30:19). That choice remains for each of us today.

Chapter 15

The Covenant Today

He has sent redemption to His people; He has ordained His Covenant forever; Holy and awesome is His name (Psalm 111:9)

Someone asked why the subject of Covenant isn't addressed from the pulpit. "It is," I replied. Every time you hear a message about love, faith, prayer, unity, protection, healing, strength, forgiveness, mercy, and faithfulness, you are hearing about one aspect of God's Covenant. It is impossible to cover the totality of Covenant in Sunday morning messages. With God's love being as multifaceted as the needs of His individual partners, even a book on the subject falls short of revealing all that He has for those who choose to walk in Covenant with Him. However, when you understand that Christianity is a Covenant, rather than a religion, you come to a profound realization. You realize that your faith can be as unshakable as Abraham's, because God still keeps His Covenant promises.

You can resist temptation as surely as Joseph did, because God still gives wisdom and strength to His Covenant partners. You can express your love as uninhibitedly as David, because God continues to extend His forgiveness and mercy to those who are called by His name. Jesus said, *"You shall know the truth and the truth shall make you free"* (John 8:32). Entering into God's Covenant and experiencing the intimacy of that relationship is the truth that sets us free—free from the bondage of the enemy, free from the lusts of our own flesh, free from divisions among ourselves, and free from the doctrines of men. We are free to walk forever in the security of God's love.

If you were a Christian prior to reading this book, it is my hope that a clearer understanding of God's Covenant has strengthened your foundation, provoked you to a deeper intimacy with the Lord, and opened your eyes to the abundant life He has made available to you. If you were searching for God at the onset of reading *The Forgotten Covenant*, it is my prayer that you have found Him, and now treasure His presence within you. Should you still be hesitant to make such a commitment, allow me to encourage you one last time.

Although God made His Covenant message so simple that even a child can understand it, misguided men with good intentions have through the years complicated the simplicity of His message. In an effort to safeguard their flocks, they impose their own requirements upon those who are seeking God. But you need not concern yourself with anyone or anything except Jesus Christ. Remember, God is listening to your heart. This is a personal moment of decision between you and the Lord.

Chapter 15

Prior to his conversion, the apostle Paul murdered Christians. Yet, when he became a believer, he said, *"Forgetting what lies behind and reaching forward to what lies ahead, I press on toward the goal for the prize of the upward call of God in Christ Jesus* (Philippians 3:113–114). God knows what has transpired in your past, and understands why you feel the way you do. *Trust Him.* He is capable of answering every question and taking care of every issue concerning you. The only decision you are required to make is the decision to come to Him. Once you make that choice, He will meet you right where you are, and never ever leave you. He will love you, give you a new heart, and place His Holy Spirit within you, to teach you, guide you, strengthen you, heal you, and protect you. As if that were not enough, when the time is right, He will take you home to be with Him forever. Left in God's hands, unsullied by human interference, God's Covenant message remains a simple roadmap home for those who choose to walk with Him.

May you receive all the blessings of the abundant life God has planned for you.

Questions, comments, or inquiries regarding speaking engagements may be addressed to:

covbook@aol.com.
or
Covenant Books
10244 Allpine Lane
St. Louis, MO 63128

The author is looking for "angels among us" type stories, which illustrate God's Covenant involvement in our everyday lives. They should be typewritten or recorded on an audio tape. Please include your name, address, phone number, and e-mail address. Send to:

Covenant Books
10244 Allpine Lane
St. Louis, MO 63128

Suggested Books Regarding Intimacy with God

The Pleasures of Loving God by Mike Bickle

The Singing God by Sam Storms

Intimate Friendship with God by Joy Dawson

The Journey of Desire by John Eldredge

The Song of the Bride by Jeanne Guyon

The Dance of the Shulamite by Barbara Urban

To order additional copies of

The Forgotten Covenant

Have your credit card ready and call:

1-877-421-READ (7323)

or please visit our web site at
www.pleasantword.com

Also available at: www.amazon.com

Printed in the United States
17349LVS00001B/271-306